Do Alliances and Partnerships Entangle the United States in Conflict?

MIRANDA PRIEBE, BRYAN ROONEY, CAITLIN MCCULLOCH, ZACHARY BURDETTE

NATIONAL SECURITY RESEARCH DIVISION

For more information on this publication, visit **www.rand.org/t/RRA739-3**.

About RAND

The RAND Corporation is a research organization that develops solutions to public policy challenges to help make communities throughout the world safer and more secure, healthier and more prosperous. RAND is nonprofit, nonpartisan, and committed to the public interest. To learn more about RAND, visit www.rand.org.

Research Integrity

Our mission to help improve policy and decisionmaking through research and analysis is enabled through our core values of quality and objectivity and our unwavering commitment to the highest level of integrity and ethical behavior. To help ensure our research and analysis are rigorous, objective, and nonpartisan, we subject our research publications to a robust and exacting quality-assurance process; avoid both the appearance and reality of financial and other conflicts of interest through staff training, project screening, and a policy of mandatory disclosure; and pursue transparency in our research engagements through our commitment to the open publication of our research findings and recommendations, disclosure of the source of funding of published research, and policies to ensure intellectual independence. For more information, visit www.rand.org/about/principles.

RAND's publications do not necessarily reflect the opinions of its research clients and sponsors.

Published by the RAND Corporation, Santa Monica, Calif.
© 2021 RAND Corporation
RAND® is a registered trademark.

Library of Congress Cataloging-in-Publication Data is available for this publication.

ISBN: 978-1-9774-0798-6

Limited Print and Electronic Distribution Rights

About This Report

The Biden administration has made strengthening U.S. alliances and partnerships a core element of its foreign policy. Yet some analysts and policymakers have raised concerns about the costs and risks associated with these relationships. In this report, we consider one aspect of the larger debate about the future of U.S. security relationships: whether they entangle the United States in wars contrary to its direct interests. This report summarizes the existing research on these questions for U.S. policymakers and offers researchers recommendations on where more research is needed to inform this debate.

This research was completed in August 2021 and conducted within the RAND Center for Analysis of U.S. Grand Strategy. The center's mission is to inform the debate about the U.S. role in the world by more clearly specifying new approaches to U.S. grand strategy, evaluating the logic of different approaches, and identifying the trade-offs each option creates. Initial funding for the center was provided by a seed grant from the Charles Koch Institute. Ongoing funding comes from RAND supporters, and from foundations and philanthropists.

RAND National Security Research Division

The center is an initiative of the International Security and Defense Policy Center of the RAND National Security Research Division (NSRD). NSRD conducts research and analysis for the Office of the Secretary of Defense, the U.S. Intelligence Community, U.S. State Department, allied foreign governments, and foundations.

For more information on the RAND Center for Analysis of U.S. Grand Strategy, see www.rand.org/nsrd/isdp/grand-strategy or contact the center director (contact information is provided on the webpage).

Acknowledgments

The authors thank Gabrielle Tarini for contributions to this report and reviewers Hal Brands and Victor Cha for thoughtful comments on an earlier draft.

Summary

Do U.S. alliances and partnerships entangle the United States in conflict up to and including war? Some strategists argue that these security relationships cause the United States to adopt its partners' interests as its own, incentivize U.S. allies and partners to engage in reckless behaviors that make conflict more likely, and risk dragging the United States into conflicts to protect its reputation for upholding its commitments. Other strategists dismiss these concerns. They contend that the United States avoids entanglement by keeping its own interests in mind and restraining its allies and partners from engaging in risky behavior.

In this report, we assess the evidence for these competing claims by examining and synthesizing the existing empirical literature. Decisions about how to manage U.S. alliances and partnerships depend on a variety of factors beyond entanglement risks, so we do not make recommendations about whether or how the United States should change its security relationships. Instead, we describe the entanglement risks associated with these relationships that should inform a holistic assessment.

Key Findings

This report is the second in a series on the security and economic trade-offs associated with competing visions for U.S. grand strategy—that is, the U.S. approach to the world. We focus on one dimension of the decision calculus about U.S. grand strategy: the risk of *entanglement*, which occurs when the United States becomes involved in a conflict because of its commitments to others rather than solely because of its own direct interests. We arrive at the following key findings:

- Entanglement dynamics contributed to, but were not the only cause of, U.S. involvement in wars in Korea, Vietnam, and Libya and in two conflicts short of war in the Taiwan Strait.

- Entanglement dynamics in these cases involved a U.S. desire to maintain its reputation with allies and adversaries for upholding its commitments or a U.S. willingness to take on allies' interests as its own.
- More research is needed on how prevalent and consequential entanglement dynamics are in U.S. decisionmaking.
- Scholars have not identified any cases of U.S. *entrapment* in war, in which the United States fought to defend an ally or partner that risked conflict because a U.S. commitment emboldened it to behave aggressively.
- The United States has allied with states that it believed posed entrapment risks, but it sought to minimize these risks through conditional alliance terms.
- Globally, states in conditional alliances have generally been less likely to initiate conflict, but U.S. alliances could still lead individual states to adopt policies that risk conflict.
- The United States has attempted to restrain allies and partners from initiating conflict in the past by leveraging military and economic aid, and it has had both successes and failures.

Contents

CHAPTER ONE

Introduction

The Biden administration sees a vast system of U.S. alliances and partnerships as a core element of its *grand strategy*, or its approach to the world.[1] President Biden has spoken about reinvesting in current alliances, maintaining an "ironclad commitment to Israel's security," and deepening relationships with such U.S. partners as India and Indonesia.[2] However, some policymakers and analysts have expressed the concern that U.S. alliances and partnerships increase the risk of the United States entering conflicts counter to its interests. Former President Trump, for example, openly questioned whether the United States should defend Montenegro, a North Atlantic Treaty Organization (NATO) ally, suggesting that such a conflict could result from Montenegrin provocation.[3] Former U.S. Ambassador to Israel Daniel B. Shapiro noted that, during negotiations over Iran's nuclear program, the Obama administration was concerned that Israel would take unilateral military action against Iran, which "could force the United States' hand to be supportive or to come in behind Israel and assist."[4] More recently,

---

[1] More specifically, *grand strategy* is "a state's logic for how it will use all of its instruments of national power to defend and promote its vital interests given international and domestic constraints" (Miranda Priebe, Bryan Rooney, Nathan Beauchamp-Mustafaga, Jeffrey Martini, and Stephanie Pezard, *Implementing Restraint: Changes in U.S. Regional Security Policies to Operationalize a Realist Grand Strategy of Restraint*, Santa Monica, Calif.: RAND Corporation, RR-A739-1, 2021, p. 1).

[2] Joseph R. Biden, Jr., "Why America Must Lead Again: Rescuing U.S. Foreign Policy After Trump," *Foreign Affairs*, Vol. 99, No. 2, March–April 2020, p. 73.

[3] Eileen Sullivan, "Trump Questions the Core of NATO: Mutual Defense, Including Montenegro," *New York Times*, July 18, 2018.

[4] Ronen Bergman and Mark Mazzetti, "The Secret History of the Push to Strike Iran," *New York Times*, last updated May 23, 2021.

some analysts have argued against proposals to make an unambiguous U.S. commitment to defend Taiwan, warning that such a commitment could embolden Taiwan's independence movement and make U.S. involvement in a war with China more likely.[5]

The risk of *entanglement*—being drawn into a conflict by virtue of a security relationship rather than solely because of national interests—is one reason that some analysts call for the United States to reevaluate the role of alliances and partnerships in its grand strategy more generally. These strategists argue that security relationships harm U.S. security by incentivizing allies and partners to take risky actions that threaten to draw the United States into conflict or by causing the United States to expand its definition of its interests.[6] Those who support maintaining or expanding U.S. security relationships tend to dismiss the risks of entanglement by arguing that commitments give the United States leverage to restrain allies from provocative behavior that can lead to conflict.[7]

---

[5]   See, for example, Bonnie S. Glaser, "Dire Straits: Should American Support for Taiwan Be Ambiguous? A Guarantee Isn't Worth the Risk," *Foreign Affairs*, September 24, 2020; and Michael J. Mazarr, "Dire Straits: Should American Support for Taiwan Be Ambiguous? A Guarantee Won't Solve the Problem," *Foreign Affairs*, September 24, 2020.

[6]   Eugene Gholz, Daryl G. Press, and Harvey M. Sapolsky, "Come Home, America: The Strategy of Restraint in the Face of Temptation," *International Security*, Vol. 21, No. 4, Spring 1997, pp. 15–19; John Glaser, Christopher A. Preble, and A. Trevor Thrall, "Towards a More Prudent American Grand Strategy," *Survival*, Vol. 61, No. 5, 2019, p. 31; Christopher Layne, *The Peace of Illusions: American Grand Strategy from 1940 to the Present*, Ithaca, N.Y.: Cornell University Press, 2007, p. 167; John J. Mearsheimer and Stephen M. Walt, "The Case for Offshore Balancing: A Superior U.S. Grand Strategy," *Foreign Affairs*, Vol. 95, No. 4, July–August 2016, p. 74; and Barry R. Posen, *Restraint: A New Foundation for U.S. Grand Strategy*, Ithaca, N.Y.: Cornell University Press, 2014, pp. 33–38. Advocates of restraint draw from Glenn H. Snyder's theoretical work on entrapment; see Glenn H. Snyder, "The Security Dilemma in Alliance Politics," *World Politics*, Vol. 36, No. 4, July 1984; and Glenn H. Snyder, *Alliance Politics*, Ithaca, N.Y.: Cornell University Press, 1997.

[7]   Hal Brands, "Rethinking America's Grand Strategy: Insights from the Cold War," *Parameters*, Vol. 45, No. 4, Winter 2015b, p. 12; Hal Brands and Peter Feaver, "Should America Retrench? The Battle over Offshore Balancing: The Risks of Retreat," *Foreign Affairs*, Vol. 95, No. 6, November–December 2016, p. 168; and Stephen G. Brooks, G. John Ikenberry, and William C. Wohlforth, "Don't Come Home, America: The Case Against Retrenchment," *International Security*, Vol. 37, No. 3, Winter 2012–2013, p. 28.

Decisions about U.S. security relationships—and U.S. grand strategy more broadly—involve several trade-offs, which the RAND Center for Analysis of U.S. Grand Strategy is analyzing in a series of reports.[8] In this second report in the series, we assess the existing evidence about one of these dimensions: the risk of entanglement associated with U.S. alliances and partnerships. Specifically, we examine the following questions:

- Does the United States attempt to mitigate entanglement risks when forming alliances and partnerships?
- How do U.S. security relationships change ally and partner incentives and conflict behavior?
- Does the United States ultimately become entangled in conflict?

We answer these questions by examining and synthesizing studies from the empirical literature on the formation and management of security relationships; alliances and conflict; and alliance restraint and entanglement. Rather than simply summarizing the findings from the literature, we assess the extent to which they apply to the three policy questions above, evaluate the methodological strengths and weaknesses of key studies, describe uncertainties that remain, and propose research that is still needed to inform debates about U.S. grand strategy.

Through our synthesis of the existing literature, we find that, in at least three cases, the United States was aware of the risk of entanglement when it was forming an alliance and sought to reduce that risk by placing conditions on its security commitments. Studies of alliances globally have found that states in such defensive conditional alliances are less likely to initiate conflict than states with other types of alliances or no alliances at all. There is less research on whether U.S. security relationships in particular are especially prone to emboldening allies and partners to adopt riskier policies that

---

[8] In this series of reports, researchers at the RAND Corporation are evaluating some of these other benefits and costs. The first report in the series considered how U.S. defense spending affects economic growth (Bryan Rooney, Grant Johnson, and Miranda Priebe, *How Does Defense Spending Affect Economic Growth?* Santa Monica, Calif.: RAND Corporation, RR-A739-2, 2021). Ongoing research in the RAND Center for Analysis of U.S. Grand Strategy is evaluating the potential economic benefits of alliances and partnerships.

make conflict more likely. We do know that the United States has had both successes and failures in its attempts to restrain allies and partners when they began to contemplate conflict. But the United States has not always defended allies and partners that became engaged in conflicts in spite of U.S. objections. Entanglement dynamics (e.g., concerns about U.S. credibility with allies and adversaries) have been factors in at least five military conflicts, including three wars, in which the United States has been involved; however, more research is needed to understand how prevalent and consequential these dynamics are because it is evident in each case that these dynamics were not the only causes of U.S. intervention. Moreover, the existing literature has not yet assessed whether and how U.S. interests expand when the United States forms a new alliance or partnership and whether this, in turn, leads the United States to become involved in more conflicts.

CHAPTER TWO

Types of U.S. Security Relationships

The United States has security relationships with many countries around the world.[1] Unfortunately, the U.S. government, journalists, and analysts often use inconsistent terms—such as *alliance, collective defense agreement,* or *partnership*—to describe this wide variety of relationships. The U.S. Department of Defense, for example, defines *allies* as states that have a security commitment from the United States that is codified in a treaty (e.g., NATO members).[2] However, U.S. law includes a *Major Non-NATO Ally* designation, which grants military and economic privileges but does not include any security commitments (e.g., Israel).[3] News reporting and policy commentary often broadly apply the term *alliance* to any country or group that has security ties to the United States (e.g., Kurdish forces in Syria).[4]

---

[1] Jennifer Kavanagh, *U.S. Security-Related Agreements in Force Since 1955: Introducing a New Database*, Santa Monica, Calif.: RAND Corporation, RR-736-AF, 2014.

[2] Claudette Roulo, "Alliances vs. Partnerships," U.S. Department of Defense, March 22, 2019. Strangely, this source also provides the example of the Moroccan-American Treaty of Peace and Friendship, a formal agreement that does not contain a security guarantee and thus does not fit the definition that the source provides. Morocco is, however, a Major Non-NATO Ally. Bureau of Near Eastern Affairs, "U.S. Relations with Morocco," fact sheet, U.S. Department of State, November 5, 2020.

[3] Some countries, such as Thailand and the Philippines, have both the Major Non-NATO Ally designation and a treaty commitment from the United States. Bureau of Political-Military Affairs, "Major Non-NATO Ally Status," fact sheet, U.S. Department of State, January 20, 2021.

[4] See, for example, Miriam Berger, "The U.S. Relationship with Ukraine Runs Deep. Here's Why," *Washington Post*, November 12, 2019; Ben Hubbard, Charlie Savage, Eric Schmitt, and Patrick Kingsley, "Abandoned by U.S. in Syria, Kurds Find New Ally in American Foe," *New York Times*, updated October 23, 2019; and Ari Shapiro, "A Look

In this report, we use the term *ally* narrowly to refer only to a country that the United States has made a treaty commitment to defend in the event of an armed attack. This category includes Japan, South Korea, and NATO allies.[5] It does not include countries that have treaties with provisions short of a U.S. defense commitment, such as Morocco, which has a treaty of friendship with the United States.

We use the term *partner* to refer to a country that has other security ties with the United States. This category includes states that engage in security cooperation with U.S. forces, receive U.S. security assistance, or host U.S. forces.[6] These ties indicate a U.S. interest in the future of these countries. The U.S. State Department, for example, notes that security cooperation with Israel is one indication that "Israel's security is a long-standing cornerstone of U.S. foreign policy."[7] In some cases, security ties are seen as a signal of an implicit U.S. commitment to defend a partner. For instance, although the United States no longer has a treaty relationship with Taiwan, the Taiwan Relations Act states that any attempt to determine the fate of Taiwan by "other than peaceful means" would be of "grave concern" to the United States.[8] The act also calls on the United States to "maintain the capacity" to defend Taiwan and to supply it with defensive military capabilities. Therefore, many analysts see the Taiwan Relations Act and long-standing security ties as constituting an implicit commitment to Taiwan's defense in at least some circumstances.[9]

---

at the History of the U.S. Alliance with the Kurds," interview with Bilal Wahab on *All Things Considered*, NPR, October 10, 2019.

[5] U.S. Department of State, "U.S. Collective Defense Arrangements," webpage, undated.

[6] See, for example, the U.S. Department of Defense's usage of the term; Roulo, 2019.

[7] Bureau of Near Eastern Affairs, "U.S. Relations with Israel," fact sheet, U.S. Department of State, January 20, 2021.

[8] Pub. L. 96-8, Taiwan Relations Act, January 1, 1979.

[9] See, for example, Robert J. Art, *A Grand Strategy for America*, Ithaca, N.Y.: Cornell University Press, 2003, p. 138; and Michael Beckley, "The Myth of Entangling Alliances: Reassessing the Security Risks of U.S. Defense Pacts," *International Security*, Vol. 39, No. 4, Spring 2015, p. 24.

In the grand strategy debate, alliances and partnerships have generally been discussed interchangeably. As we will describe, however, empirical research has often focused on alliances rather than partnerships. We therefore distinguish between the two types of security relationships as appropriate when discussing the evidence throughout this report.

CHAPTER THREE

Defining *Entanglement*

We define *entanglement* as a situation in which a state enters a conflict because of the presence of a security relationship. The key criterion here is that the state must support the ally *because of the security relationship* rather than only because of its own intrinsic interests in the dispute. Evidence of entanglement at work could include, for example, policymakers arguing that war is not directly in the U.S. interest but that the United States must intervene to show its allies, partners, or adversaries its willingness to uphold commitments or because of a moral or legal obligation to defend its allies.[1]

Historically, the United States has supported and even fought to defend other countries for many reasons other than entanglement. For example, the United States fought in World War I on the side of countries, such as Britain and France, that were not allies or partners at the time. Furthermore, not all conflicts involving allies and partners constitute entanglement. After all, the United States often forms these relationships because it sees an interest in a country's future. Even if the United States had not formed an alliance with West Germany during the Cold War, it still might have fought to prevent a Soviet occupation, which would have given the Soviets control of significant industrial capacity in Europe. The key question for identifying

---

[1] Our use of *entanglement* and *entrapment* follows Tongfi Kim, "Why Alliances Entangle but Seldom Entrap States," *Security Studies*, Vol. 20, No. 3, 2011, p. 355. Snyder's broad definition of *entrapment* as "being dragged into a conflict over an ally's interests that one does not share, or shares only partially" aligns with our definition of *entanglement* (Snyder, 1984, p. 467).

cases of entanglement is whether the United States would have intervened for its own interest even if there were no alliance.[2]

We examine entanglement in all types of conflicts between states, including full-scale wars as well as conflicts short of war, such as explicit military threats, displays of force, and small skirmishes.[3] Although entanglement in war carries the greatest consequences, understanding whether security relationships draw the United States into lower levels of conflict is also important. Low-level disputes can fuel insecurity and competition, which might then escalate into war or create costs by undermining cooperation and encouraging arms racing.[4]

Analysts often conflate entanglement with entrapment. *Entrapment* is a form of entanglement in which a state "adopts a *risky or offensive* policy not specified in the alliance agreement" that pulls another state into a conflict

---

[2] *Chain-ganging* is an extreme form of this dynamic. In certain contexts, a state's security might depend on the survival of other great powers. The state might then feel compelled to defend another power even if there is no alliance. Chain-ganging is distinct from entanglement because the motivation for the state to intervene comes from the distribution of power and the threat to its own survival rather than alliance concerns (e.g., reputation or allied reassurance). Kim, 2011, pp. 357–358. For a more in-depth discussion of chain-ganging, see Thomas J. Christensen and Jack Snyder, "Chain Gangs and Passed Bucks: Predicting Alliance Patterns in Multipolarity," *International Organization*, Vol. 44, No. 2, Spring 1990. Theoretically, multipolar systems might be especially prone to emboldenment because states believe that their coalition partners have little choice but to come to their aid. In this sense, a logic similar to entrapment could exist even in the absence of an alliance or a partnership. For a discussion of these dynamics in multipolarity, see Snyder, 1997, pp. 187–188.

[3] The militarized interstate dispute (MID) data set, which political scientists commonly use in the study of conflict, defines an *interstate war* as "a series of sustained battles between the armed forces of two or more states that result in a total of 1,000 battle-deaths" (Zeev Maoz, Paul L. Johnson, Jasper Kaplan, Fiona Ogunkoya, and Aaron Shreve, *Dyadic MID Codebook—Version 4.02*, Davis, Calif.: Department of Political Science, University of California, Davis, June 18, 2021, p. 3). Threats, displays, or uses of force that do not rise to this threshold are considered MIDs but not interstate wars. We refer to this range of militarized disputes below the conventional threshold for interstate war as *conflicts short of war* rather than *lower-level MIDs*.

[4] See Michael P. Colaresi and William R. Thompson, "Hot Spots or Hot Hands? Serial Crisis Behavior, Escalating Risks, and Rivalry," *Journal of Politics*, Vol. 64, No. 4, November 2002; and Paul D. Senese and John A. Vasquez, *The Steps to War: An Empirical Study*, Princeton, N.J.: Princeton University Press, 2008.

that it would not have fought absent the existence of the alliance or partnership.[5] Examples of such policies include taking provocative actions aimed at extracting concessions from an adversary, refusing to compromise over a dispute, and even initiating a war.[6] Entrapment is, therefore, a narrow concept that is only one possible form of entanglement.

There are other, related topics that we do not consider in this report. For instance, U.S. alliances and partnerships can deter adversaries from initiating conflicts or, conversely, can provoke adversaries in ways that lead to conflicts.[7] Some analysts argue that security ties with the United States can also entangle other states in U.S.-led operations, which is effectively the reverse of the dynamic that we discuss in this report.[8] Scholars have also considered the extent to which U.S. alliances and partnerships have prevented nuclear proliferation.[9] These issues cover only some of the potential

---

[5]   Kim, 2011, p. 355 (emphasis in original).

[6]   Snyder, 1997, p. 183.

[7]   For contrasting views on the effects of alliances on deterring attacks on alliance members, see Michael R. Kenwick, John A. Vasquez, and Matthew A. Powers, "Do Alliances Really Deter?" *Journal of Politics*, Vol. 77, No. 4, October 2015; and Brett Ashley Leeds, "Do Alliances Deter Aggression? The Influence of Military Alliances on the Initiation of Militarized Interstate Disputes," *American Journal of Political Science*, Vol. 47, No. 3, July 2003.

[8]   For evidence that U.S. alliances entangle at least some weaker allies, see Andrés J. Gannon and Daniel Kent, "Keeping Your Friends Close, but Acquaintances Closer: Why Weakly Allied States Make Committed Coalition Partners," *Journal of Conflict Resolution*, Vol. 65, No. 5, 2021. For evidence that side payments, not just alliance relationships, have secured contributions to U.S. operations, see Marina E. Henke, "Buying Allies: Payment Practices in Multilateral Military Coalition-Building," *International Security*, Vol. 43, No. 4, Spring 2019b. For an argument that the value of allied participation is often more symbolic than militarily significant, see Sarah E. Kreps, *Coalitions of Convenience: United States Military Interventions After the Cold War*, Cambridge, UK: Oxford University Press, 2011.

[9]   On U.S. attempts to leverage economic and security ties to prevent nuclear proliferation, see Philipp C. Bleek and Eric B. Lorber, "Security Guarantees and Allied Nuclear Proliferation," *Journal of Conflict Resolution*, Vol. 58, No. 3, April 2014; Francis J. Gavin, "Strategies of Inhibition: U.S. Grand Strategy, the Nuclear Revolution, and Nonproliferation," *International Security*, Vol. 40, No. 1, Summer 2015; Gene Gerzhoy, "Alliance Coercion and Nuclear Restraint: How the United States Thwarted West Germany's Nuclear Ambitions," *International Security*, Vol. 39, No. 4, Spring 2015; Alexander

costs and benefits of alliances that merit consideration as part of a broader assessment of how the United States should approach alliances and partnerships in the future. The risk of U.S. entanglement that we examine in this report is only one dimension of this broader calculation.

Lanoszka, *Atomic Assurance: The Alliance Politics of Nuclear Proliferation*, Ithaca, N.Y.: Cornell University Press, 2018a; Nicholas L. Miller, "The Secret Success of Nonproliferation Sanctions," *International Organization*, Vol. 68, No. 4, Fall 2014; and Nicholas L. Miller, *Stopping the Bomb: The Sources and Effectiveness of US Nonproliferation Policy*, Ithaca, N.Y.: Cornell University Press, 2018. Research has shown that U.S. willingness to pressure allies and partners on nonproliferation has changed over time and that success has also varied; see Miller, 2014, p. 914; Miller, 2018, pp. 20–28, 148; and Or Rabinowitz and Nicholas L. Miller, "Keeping the Bombs in the Basement: U.S. Nonproliferation Policy Toward Israel, South Africa, and Pakistan," *International Security*, Vol. 40, No. 1, Summer 2015.

CHAPTER FOUR

Competing Claims About Security Relationships and Entanglement

In this chapter, we introduce two prominent schools of thought about U.S. grand strategy and the competing claims they make about entanglement.

Claims That Alliances and Partnerships Entangle

Advocates of a grand strategy of restraint or offshore balancing, also known as *restrainers*, call for greater emphasis on diplomacy and less U.S. military engagement abroad. These strategists call for reduced forward military presence, a higher bar for the use of force, and negotiations to settle conflicts of interest with U.S. adversaries diplomatically. They argue that the United States should stop expanding its alliances, renegotiate alliances to reduce entanglement risks, or even end some of its existing alliances and partnerships.

Fear of entanglement is one of the reasons that advocates of restraint say the United States should reexamine its security relationships.[1] This is not to say that all restrainers believe that the United States should end all existing commitments. Rather, many of these strategists argue that the United States should keep its security commitments limited to states that help protect vital U.S. interests and should take steps to mitigate entanglement risks.

---

[1] Advocates of restraint also argue that U.S. security relationships and the way in which the United States manages them disincentivize allies and partners from spending on their own defense, provoke adversaries unnecessarily, and create an unsustainable level of U.S. defense spending. For an overview of this approach to grand strategy, see Priebe et al., 2021.

For example, some restrainers have called for maintaining the U.S. alliance with Japan to balance against China but have advocated for renegotiating the alliance terms so that Japan does more for its own defense.[2]

Advocates of restraint highlight three ways in which alliances entangle. First, allies and partners might see a U.S. security commitment as evidence that the United States will defend them regardless of how a conflict begins. This belief in an unconditional U.S. commitment could embolden allies and partners to adopt policies that make a conflict more likely because they think they have a "blank check" to bankroll aggressive policies. As one group of restrainers put it,

> When someone else is going to pay the price for an ill-advised action—
> that is, when the United States is going to come "fix" any predicament
> that its allies get into—there is little incentive to avoid trouble. It is easy
> to gamble with someone else's money.[3]

Restrainers express the fear that, if a crisis escalates, the United States might feel compelled to defend the reckless ally or partner because it believes that its own credibility is on the line, so failing to act could cause other allies and adversaries to question U.S. commitments elsewhere.[4] This combination of ally emboldenment and U.S. intervention to defend the ally constitutes entrapment.

Advocates of restraint often present entrapment as a general risk that is associated with U.S. security relationships. They have not made any explicit distinctions between alliances and partnerships as we do here. These strategists have pointed to the potential entrapment risks associated with the U.S. alliances with Japan, the Philippines, and Eastern European and Baltic

---

[2] See, for example, Posen, 2014.

[3] Gholz, Press, and Sapolsky, 1997, p. 16.

[4] For references to entrapment risks by advocates of restraint, see, for example, Gholz, Press, and Sapolsky, 1997, p. 15; Layne, 2007, p. 169; Barry R. Posen, "Pull Back: The Case for a Less Activist Foreign Policy," *Foreign Affairs,* Vol. 92, No. 1, January–February 2013; and Posen, 2014, pp. 33, 44. Our more detailed explanation of the logic of entrapment draws on Snyder, 1997, pp. 181–183.

allies in NATO.[5] Restrainers also see risks in relationships with U.S. partners, such as Taiwan and Georgia. They argue that Taiwan's leaders would have been more cautious in their rhetoric about independence in the past if Taiwan had not had a long-standing security relationship with the United States. Advocates of restraint also claim that expectations of U.S. support led Georgia to adopt provocative policies toward South Ossetia in 2008, which led to war with Russia. Although the United States was not drawn into this conflict, restrainers argue that the case highlights how U.S. security relationships incentivize risk-taking by allies and partners.[6]

Second, alliances can entangle if the United States sees its credibility— specifically, its reputation for upholding its commitments—as being on the line in a wider variety of issues involving its allies and partners.[7] Even though a U.S. commitment might be narrow, such as defending the ally's homeland in the event of an attack, the United States might worry that other allies and adversaries see a U.S. response to any issue involving the ally as an indication of U.S. commitment in different contexts. The United States might come to believe that, to protect its credibility, it has to fight wars over peripheral interests involving U.S. allies both to reassure allies and to deter

---

[5] On entrapment risks in Asia, see Ted Galen Carpenter, "It's Time to Suspend America's Alliance with the Philippines," *National Interest*, October 1, 2016; Doug Bandow, "The U.S. Doesn't Need the Philippines," *New York Times*, updated October 18, 2016; David M. Edelstein and Joshua R. Itzkowitz Shifrinson, "It's a Trap! Security Commitments and the Risks of Entrapment," in A. Trevor Thrall and Benjamin H. Friedman, eds., *US Grand Strategy in the 21st Century*, London: Routledge, 2018, p. 36; and John Glaser, "Withdrawing from Overseas Bases: Why a Forward-Deployed Military Posture Is Unnecessary, Outdated, and Dangerous," Washington, D.C.: Cato Institute, Policy Analysis No. 816, July 18, 2017. On entrapment risks in NATO, see Emma Ashford, "Power and Pragmatism: Reforming American Foreign Policy for the 21st Century," in Richard Fontaine and Loren DeJonge Schulman, eds., *New Voices in Grand Strategy*, Washington, D.C.: Center for a New American Security, 2019, pp. 8–9. On entanglement risks associated with arms sales, see A. Trevor Thrall and Caroline Dorminey, *Risky Business: The Role of Arms Sales in U.S. Foreign Policy*, Washington, D.C.: Cato Institute, Policy Analysis No. 836, March 13, 2018.

[6] Benjamin H. Friedman, "Bad Idea: Permanent Alliances," Defense360, December 13, 2018; and Posen, 2013. For concerns about entrapment risks associated with the U.S. relationship with Taiwan specifically, see Ted Galen Carpenter, *America's Coming War with China: A Collision Course over Taiwan*, New York: Palgrave MacMillan, 2005.

[7] Posen, 2014, p. 44.

adversaries. Entanglement dynamics do not have to involve the ally or partner that the United States is defending. Rather, entanglement would be at work if the United States were to become involved in conflict to show its reliability to other allies and partners who might be watching. These mechanisms could result in the United States risking or fighting wars that it would not have considered absent the alliance or partnership.[8]

Third, once the United States makes a security commitment, it might begin to define its interests more expansively, effectively adopting the ally's or partner's interests as its own. Diplomatic and military interactions with the ally might cause the United States to become socialized to its concerns. Even having a seat at the table with U.S. leaders could give states opportunities to influence U.S. choices. Domestic lobbying by allies and partners might further socialize the U.S. public or policymakers to ally and partner concerns. Through lobbying, these allies and partners could create a constituency within the United States that promotes military involvement in a wider variety of issues involving those states.[9]

Restrainers also note that there are forms of entanglement that remain short of U.S. involvement in military conflict, which we do not evaluate in this report. Edelstein and Itzkowitz Shifrinson argue that entanglement dynamics in Asia have affected U.S. force levels and the way the United States approaches its relationship with China.[10] Posen uses the term *reckless driving* to refer to allies and partners that adopt riskier policies of all kinds because of an expectation of continued U.S. support. For example, Posen argues that U.S. military aid and political support have freed up resources for Israel to spend on settlement activities in the West Bank. The U.S. association with Israel's policies on settlements and toward the Palestinians

---

[8]   Thrall and Dorminey, 2018.

[9]   Layne, 2007, p. 131; Stephen M. Walt, *Taming American Power: The Global Response to U.S. Primacy*, New York: W. W. Norton & Company, 2006, pp. 191–217; and Stephen M. Walt, "How to Tell If You're in a Good Alliance," *Foreign Policy*, October 28, 2019. Scholars outside the grand strategy debate have also suggested some of these dynamics. See, for example, Beckley, 2015, p. 13; Robert O. Keohane, "The Big Influence of Small Allies," *Foreign Policy*, No. 2, Spring 1971; and James D. Morrow, "Alliances: Why Write Them Down?" *Annual Review of Political Science*, Vol. 3, No. 1, 2000.

[10]   Edelstein and Itzkowitz Shifrinson, 2018.

more generally, Posen argues, has harmed U.S. standing in the Arab world and has undercut its foreign policy goals with these countries, including counterterrorism.[11]

Claims That Alliances and Partnerships Do Not Entangle

There are many strategists who support maintaining or even expanding U.S. alliances and partnerships. Although there are differences among such strategies as deep engagement, selective engagement, and primacy, these strategies broadly support these relationships and other key elements of U.S. grand strategy since the end of the Cold War, including a sizable forward U.S. military presence and more military interventions abroad than advocates of restraint support.[12] We refer to this group collectively as *advocates of U.S. military engagement.*

These strategists tend to reject concerns about entanglement and argue instead that security relationships give the United States leverage to restrain allies and partners from provoking or initiating conflicts. Advocates of U.S. military engagement claim that the United States can choose not to offer an alliance to a state that presents entanglement risks in the first place.[13]

---

[11] Posen, 2014, pp. 44–50, 66.

[12] Robert J. Art, "Selective Engagement in the Era of Austerity," in Richard Fontaine and Kristin M. Lord, eds., *America's Path: Grand Strategy for the Next Administration*, Washington, D.C.: Center for a New American Security, May 2012; Hal Brands, "Choosing Primacy: U.S. Strategy and Global Order at the Dawn of the Post–Cold War Era," *Texas National Security Review*, Vol. 1, No. 2, February 2018; Brooks, Ikenberry, and Wohlforth, 2012; and Stephen G. Brooks and William C. Wohlforth, *America Abroad: The United States' Global Role in the 21st Century*, New York: Oxford University Press, 2016. See also the discussion of alliances in Mira Rapp-Hooper, *Shields of the Republic: The Triumph and Peril of America's Alliances*, Cambridge, Mass.: Harvard University Press, 2020, pp. 85–92.

[13] Stephen G. Brooks, G. John Ikenberry, and William C. Wohlforth, "Lean Forward: In Defense of American Engagement," *Foreign Affairs*, Vol. 92, No. 1, January–February 2013, p. 136; and Alexander Lanoszka, "Do Allies Really Free Ride?" *Survival*, Vol. 57, No. 3, 2015.

Once a security relationship is formed, the potential for the United States to withdraw support can dissuade allies and partners from acting recklessly for two reasons.[14] First, all U.S. alliances have conditional alliance terms. Completely unconditional alliance commitments would obligate a state to aid an ally whenever the ally becomes involved in a war—a true blank check—whereas conditional alliances trigger the commitment only under certain circumstances or give allies more latitude to decide how to respond. The United States only has defensive conditional alliances.[15] This means that the United States can threaten to stay out of the conflict without breaking its promises. In this way, these strategists argue, U.S. credibility with adversaries or other allies will not suffer if the United States chooses not to support a reckless ally.[16]

Second, these strategists argue that U.S. allies are dependent on the United States for security. The United States can refuse support in a particular crisis, withdraw U.S. forces, end military aid, or, in the extreme, end the security relationship all together. This means that the United States has leverage to pressure allies to abandon provocative policies or to accept terms with an adversary to avoid conflict.[17] Because the United States is powerful and its survival does not hinge on any particular ally, it can more credibly

---

[14] Brands, 2015b, p. 12; Brands and Feaver, 2016, p. 168; Brooks, Ikenberry, and Wohlforth, 2012, p. 28; Brooks and Wohlforth, 2016. For an example of this argument applied to Taiwan, see Richard Haass and David Sacks, "American Support for Taiwan Must Be Unambiguous: To Keep the Peace, Make Clear to China That Force Won't Stand," *Foreign Affairs*, September 2, 2020.

[15] Brett V. Benson, "Unpacking Alliances: Deterrent and Compellent Alliances and Their Relationship with Conflict, 1816–2000," *Journal of Politics*, Vol. 73, No. 4, October 2011.

[16] Benson, 2011.

[17] Hal Brands, "Fools Rush Out? The Flawed Logic of Offshore Balancing," *Washington Quarterly*, Vol. 38, No. 2, 2015a. Not all advocates of deep engagement focus on U.S. power advantages. Beckley, 2015, explains situations in which U.S. allies successfully restrained the United States despite being relatively weaker. See also Victor D. Cha, *Powerplay: The Origins of the American Alliance System in Asia*, Princeton, N.J.: Princeton University Press, 2016, p. 26; Robert Kagan, "Superpowers Don't Get to Retire," *New Republic*, May 26, 2014; and Rapp-Hooper, 2020.

make such threats and sidestep costly conflicts when its vital interests are not at stake.[18]

Advocates of military engagement also generally reject the argument that alliances and partnerships cause U.S. interests to expand. They counter that shared interests drive the United States to form security relationships. Brands and Feaver argue that "alliances do not cause US entanglements overseas; entanglements cause alliances."[19] Rather than changing the U.S. conception of its national interests, these relationships reflect U.S. interests that exist separately from the alliances and led to their creation. If U.S. interests and an ally's interests do start to diverge over time, the ally's dependence on the United States might make it more likely to shift its own policies to maintain the relationship rather than the other way around.[20]

Finally, the diversity of U.S. alliances may limit entanglement risks because each ally has incentives to restrain the United States from expending its power in interventions to support other allies. Allies in one region act as a check on any U.S. temptation to embroil itself in conflicts in other regions because of credibility concerns or socialization.[21] For example, European states might pressure the United States to avoid becoming entangled in a conflict in Asia because it could undermine the U.S. ability to deter Russia.[22]

In summary, advocates of restraint argue that alliances and partnerships may entangle the United States in war if they embolden allies and partners or cause the United States to worry about its credibility or expand its conception of its interests. Conversely, advocates of military engagement argue that the United States has leverage to restrain its allies and partners and to secure their support for broader U.S. interests because they are dependent on the United States for economic and military support.

---

[18] Beckley, 2015, p. 18.

[19] Hal Brands and Peter D. Feaver, "What Are America's Alliances Good For?" *Parameters*, Vol. 47, No. 2, Summer 2017, p. 18.

[20] Brooks and Wohlforth, 2016, pp. 91–93.

[21] Beckley, 2015, p. 20.

[22] For a detailed analysis of allied reactions to U.S. involvement in the First Taiwan Strait Crisis (1954–1955), see Iain D. Henry, "What Allies Want: Reconsidering Loyalty, Reliability, and Alliance Interdependence," *International Security*, Vol. 44, No. 4, Spring 2020.

Because claims about entanglement rest on several supporting assumptions, we consider the evidence for each issue in turn. In Chapter Five, we consider how entanglement risks affect U.S. decisions about how to choose its allies and partners and how to structure the terms of its relationships with them. In Chapter Six, we discuss how an alliance or partnership, once formed, affects allied incentives and conflict behavior. Finally, in Chapter Seven, we assess whether the United States ultimately becomes entangled in conflict.

CHAPTER FIVE

Does the United States Try to Mitigate Entanglement Risks When Forming Alliances and Partnerships?

There are many factors that states consider when forming an alliance or partnership.[1] Entanglement risks might be one of these considerations. All things being equal, states might wish to avoid forming security relationships with states known for provocative behavior or, failing that, to place limits or conditions on the commitment. That said, entanglement concerns might not always be paramount. In the face of a significant threat, for example, a state might form an alliance even if it has concerns about the ally's wider ambitions or risk-taking.

Our review of the literature found that there has not been an assessment of how entanglement concerns have generally affected the U.S. choice of allies or partners in practice. There has, however, been in-depth research on three individual cases. These studies found that the United States promoted West Germany's entry to NATO and formed alliances with South Korea and Taiwan in the 1950s despite—and partly because of—entanglement concerns.[2] The United States and its NATO allies worried about German militarism, including the risk that West Germany might one day seek to

---

[1]   See, for example, Michaela Mattes, "Reputation, Symmetry, and Alliance Design," *International Organization*, Vol. 66, No. 4, Fall 2012; Morrow, 2000; and Stephen M. Walt, *The Origins of Alliance*, Ithaca, N.Y.: Cornell University Press, 1987.

[2]   Cha, 2016; and Marc Trachtenberg, *A Constructed Peace: The Making of the European Settlement, 1945–1963*, Vol. 79, Princeton, N.J.: Princeton University Press, 1999, pp. 125–128.

forcibly reunify with East Germany.[3] In this period, the United States also worried that the Republic of China (ROC) on Taiwan, which openly sought to retake control of the Chinese mainland, would pull the United States into the Chinese Civil War.[4] Similarly, the United States worried that South Korean President Syngman Rhee, who had long hoped to unify the Korean Peninsula, would restart hostilities with North Korea after the armistice in 1953.[5] Although the United States did not want these partners to pull it into a war, the United States cared about their futures and, in particular, did not want them to fall to communism. In fact, U.S. leaders viewed an alliance as helping the United States avoid entanglement better than only informal partnerships in each of these cases, as we discuss below.[6] This evidence suggests that entrapment concerns are not, on their own, disqualifying for a U.S. alliance. However, without a systematic review, it is difficult to know how entrapment concerns have affected U.S. alliance and partnership choices more generally.[7]

We next consider whether the United States has tried to reduce the risk of entanglement through the negotiation of conditional alliance terms. The North Atlantic Treaty is an example of a conditional defense agreement because it does not require an automatic response to an attack on a NATO member. Rather, Article 5 of the treaty calls on each member to take "such action as it deems necessary" if another member is attacked.[8] This choice of

---

[3] Trachtenberg, 1999, pp. 125–128.

[4] Jeremy Pressman, *Warring Friends: Alliance Restraint in International Politics,* Ithaca, N.Y.: Cornell University Press, 2008, p. 35.

[5] Claudia J. Kim, "Military Alliances as a Stabilising Force: U.S. Relations with South Korea and Taiwan, 1950s–1960s," *Journal of Strategic Studies,* Vol. 42, 2019.

[6] Victor D. Cha, "Powerplay: Origins of the U.S. Alliance System in Asia," *International Security,* Vol. 34, No. 3, Winter 2009–2010, p. 170; Kim, 2019.

[7] A recent review of U.S. decisions not to ally with Israel between 1961 and 1973 did not highlight entrapment concerns. It pointed instead to concerns about the effects that such a treaty would have on U.S. relationships with other states in the region and a perception that Israel could adequately defend itself. Keren Yarhi-Milo, Alexander Lanoszka, and Zack Cooper, "To Arm or to Ally? The Patron's Dilemma and the Strategic Logic of Arms Transfers and Alliances," *International Security,* Vol. 41, No. 2, Fall 2016.

[8] NATO, North Atlantic Treaty, April 4, 1949.

wording stemmed, at least in part, from U.S. congressional concerns that earlier drafts contained language that interfered with Congress's constitutional power to declare war.[9] The North Atlantic Treaty is also geographically limited to Europe and North America and does not include, for example, commitments to defend against attacks on allies' colonial holdings.[10] As noted earlier, all U.S. alliances are conditional, although the degree and nature of conditionality vary.[11]

There has not been an examination of all U.S. alliance agreements to determine to what extent entanglement, sovereignty, or other concerns drove the choice to make these commitments conditional.[12] However, there is evidence that, during the 1950s, concerns about entanglement affected the alliance terms that the United States was willing to accept in its negotiations with Taiwan, South Korea, and West Germany. The Eisenhower administration would agree to the now-defunct Mutual Defense Treaty with Taiwan in 1954 only if the ROC pledged to limit all operations against the Chinese mainland to those that the United States approved in advance. A secret addendum to the treaty codified this. As a further hedge against entrapment, the treaty explicitly committed the United States to defend only

---

[9] Timothy Andrews Sayle, *Enduring Alliance: A History of NATO and the Postwar Global Order*, Ithaca, N.Y.: Cornell University Press, 2019, pp. 16–17.

[10] NATO, 1949. Beyond the treaty language itself, Sayle documents early U.S. resistance to discussing global security issues in the NATO forum; Sayle, 2019, pp. 18, 28–29, 33.

[11] The data code U.S. alliances as conditional in Benson, 2011, and in Brett Leeds, Jeffrey Ritter, Sara Mitchell, and Andrew Long, "Alliance Treaty Obligations and Provisions, 1815–1944," *International Interactions*, Vol. 28, No. 3, 2002.

[12] The U.S. choice of conditional alliances might be overdetermined, since the U.S. Constitution grants Congress the authority to declare war. Therefore, U.S. leaders would not likely gain Senate approval to enter into alliances that precommit the United States to fight in hypothetical future wars. The United States is not alone in its preference for conditional alliances, however. Scholars have found that democracies frequently design conditional alliances. Daina Chiba, Jesse C. Johnson, and Brett Ashley Leeds, "Careful Commitments: Democratic States and Alliance Design," *Journal of Politics*, Vol. 77, No. 4, October 2015.

the islands of Taiwan and Penghu. The United States intentionally left the treaty's applicability to other ROC-controlled islands ambiguous.[13]

The United States also sought to mitigate entrapment risks when negotiating its alliance with South Korea. South Korea's national policy at the time was "unification by marching north," which President Rhee privately referred to as "unification or death!"[14] During the Korean War, Rhee also took provocative measures aimed at sabotaging armistice talks and restarting hostilities.[15] While negotiating the defense treaty, U.S. leaders told Rhee that the United States would not assist South Korea if it were the aggressor.[16] South Korea repeatedly sought stronger language to signal firmer U.S. commitments, while the United States steadfastly refused those requests.[17] A subsequent memorandum of understanding also gave the United States operational control over South Korean forces, which the United States sought in part to strengthen its ability to restrain South Korea.[18]

The United States and its NATO allies also saw an alliance as part of the solution for both restraining and protecting West Germany, which they viewed as fundamental to their security. During 1954, a series of interrelated agreements, known as the Paris Accords, provided for the end of the occupation of West Germany, its rearmament, and its admission to NATO. The United States and its allies wanted West Germany to rearm to balance

---

[13] Cha, 2009, pp. 170–171; Thomas J. Christensen, *Worse Than a Monolith: Alliance Politics and Problems of Coercive Diplomacy in Asia*, Princeton, N.J.: Princeton University Press, 2011, p. 143; and Pressman, 2008, pp. 33–36.

[14] Cha, 2016, p. 94.

[15] Cha, 2016, pp. 101–104.

[16] Cha, 2009, pp. 175–176; Cha, 2016, pp. 110–113; Kim, 2011; Kim, 2019.

[17] Kim, 2019, p. 8.

[18] Cha, 2009, p. 176. In 1994, the United States returned peacetime operational control to South Korea, but it was still obligated to command combined U.S.–South Korean forces in the event of war. In 2007, at Seoul's request, Washington agreed in principle to return wartime operational control to South Korea. Since that time, the allies have been preparing to transfer operational control to a combined command led by a South Korean general with a U.S. deputy. Emma Chanlett-Avery, *U.S.–South Korea Alliance: Issues for Congress*, Washington, D.C.: Congressional Research Service, IF11388, Version 2, updated June 23, 2020; and Choe Sang-Hun, "U.S. and South Korea Agree to Delay Shift in Wartime Command," *New York Times*, October 24, 2014.

against the Soviet Union, but it also sought limits on how Germany could use its military power after its role in earlier European wars. The agreements allowed U.S. and other NATO members' military forces to remain in West Germany and required the integration of Western German military forces into NATO's command structure. These two provisions sought to give foreign governments greater control over how West German military power was used and to prevent West German forces from operating—and therefore starting a war—independently. West Germany also promised not to seek reunification with East Germany or otherwise change its boundaries by force.[19]

There is at least one example of the United States worrying about entanglement concerns in the context of a partnership. The United States ended its alliance with Taiwan when it normalized relations with the People's Republic of China (PRC). The terms of the 1979 Taiwan Relations Act, which now governs the U.S. partnership with Taiwan, do not include an explicit commitment to Taiwan's defense in the event of war.[20] By formally committing only to selling Taiwan defensive arms and having the capability to defend Taiwan, the United States sought to maintain strategic ambiguity.[21] This was in part because the United States hoped that uncertainty about when or whether it would defend Taiwan would prevent the ROC from adopting provocative policies toward China that would entrap the United States in a war.[22] Other U.S. partnerships are also ambiguous in that there is no formal commitment. However, there has not been research on whether the United States has avoided alliance commitments in some of these other cases because of entanglement concerns or whether it set terms for these partnerships that would address entanglement risks.

---

[19] Trachtenberg, 1999, pp. 125–128.

[20] Pub. L. 96-8, 1979.

[21] Alan D. Romberg, *Rein In at the Brink of the Precipice: American Policy Toward Taiwan and U.S.-PRC Relations*, Washington, D.C.: Henry L. Stimson Center, 2003, p. 173.

[22] Even U.S. pledges to Taiwan of security support short of an alliance have drawn military threats from China. "China Warns Taiwan Independence 'Means War' as US Pledges Support," BBC News, January 29, 2021.

In sum, the United States has formed alliances with states known to have revisionist ambitions in at least two cases—South Korea and Taiwan—and allowed West Germany's entry into NATO despite concerns that it would develop wider aims in the future. In each case, the United States sought specific alliance terms that were intended to reduce entrapment risks. It is unclear to what extent entanglement concerns affected deliberations about U.S. alliances and partnerships more generally. For its partnerships, the United States does not make a stated commitment at all, which also means that it is not formally committed to defend partners that engage in risky behavior. Still, it would be helpful to know more about whether the United States takes other steps to reduce entanglement risks in these relationships.

Although the United States might hope that conditional alliance terms and partnerships without formal commitments reduce entanglement risks, that might not be the case. After all, conditionality might not alter behavior if the ally or partner does not actually believe that U.S. support is conditional. Steps that the United States takes throughout the life of a security relationship to reassure an ally or partner, for example, could suggest a very strong U.S. commitment. Therefore, in the next chapter, we discuss how alliances and partnerships, once formed, affect the perceptions and conflict behavior of U.S. allies and partners.

CHAPTER SIX

How Do U.S. Security Relationships Change Ally and Partner Incentives and Conflict Behavior?

Advocates of restraint argue that U.S. security commitments embolden allies and partners to adopt riskier policies that make conflict more likely. Conversely, advocates of U.S. military engagement argue that the United States can restrain allies and partners from provoking conflict. We consider these two claims about ally motivations and U.S. influence in turn. The qualitative literature that examines the U.S. experience with emboldenment and restraint is limited and cannot suggest which of these dynamics might dominate, so we also consider the quantitative literature on how defensive alliances beyond the U.S. alliance network affect conflict behavior.

Does Having a U.S. Security Relationship Embolden States to Pursue Policies That Make Conflict More Likely?

Studying ally emboldenment and self-restraint is challenging for several reasons. First, whenever scholars seek to discern a state's motivations, they prefer to have detailed information about its decisionmaking, not just its behavior—but records of internal deliberations are not always available. Second, even with such records, it can be difficult to confirm or disprove emboldenment. Scholars would ideally find evidence in the documentary record that allies or partners made calculations about U.S. support when choosing policies that risked conflict, but the expectation of U.S. support could be an assumption that decisionmakers did not state explicitly. Finally, states might have pursued policies that risked conflict even if they did not have the United States to fall back on. Therefore, research on emboldenment needs to consider these alternative explanations for ally and partner choices.

It is also difficult to know how often U.S. allies and partners have been more restrained in their behavior toward an adversary because of U.S. security commitments, since such cases would not produce the crises that researchers are more likely to study. Despite these challenges, scholars can often find ways to systematically study questions about state motivations. Unfortunately, ally and partner emboldenment and self-restraint have not been a focus of scholarly research.

The few cases that have received attention illustrate the methodological challenges. For example, analysts have asked whether Georgia's behavior in 2008 was a case of U.S. support driving partner risk-taking. Prior to the crisis with Russia over the separatist regions of South Ossetia and Abkhazia, the United States had supported Georgia's membership to NATO and had provided military assistance.[1] As tensions between Russia and Georgia increased, U.S. Secretary of State Condoleezza Rice went to Georgia and cautioned it against using force.[2] However, she also reaffirmed the U.S. commitment to Georgia's territorial integrity. Furthermore, in response to a question about Israel, another U.S. partner, Secretary Rice stressed that the United States "take[s] very strongly our obligation to defend our allies, and nobody should be confused about that."[3] These mixed messages, along with previous indications of U.S. support, could potentially have convinced Georgia that the United States was likely to support it in further action

---

[1] After Georgia's progression toward membership failed at a NATO summit in 2008, U.S. and NATO leaders still visited Georgia and spoke positively about the relationship. Alexander Lanoszka, "Tangled Up in Rose? Theories of Alliance Entrapment and the 2008 Russo-Georgian War," *Contemporary Security Policy*, Vol. 39, No. 2, 2018b, p. 245.

[2] Alexander Cooley and Daniel Nexon, "Interpersonal Networks and International Security," in Deborah Avant and Oliver Westerwinter, eds., *The New Power Politics: Networks and Transnational Security Governance*, New York: Oxford University Press, 2016.

[3] Gerard Toal, *Near Abroad: Putin, the West, and the Contest over Ukraine and the Caucasus*, Oxford, UK: Oxford University Press, 2017, p. 157. This was in a statement to both the Russian and the Georgian media.

against Russia, in spite of U.S. warnings.[4] Although this claim is plausible, there is no direct evidence about what motivated Georgian decisionmaking. One detailed study found that the evidence about the role of expectations of U.S. support in Georgian decisionmaking is limited and inconclusive.[5]

Similarly, some analysts have argued that the U.S. partnership, and, later, alliance, with the ROC in the 1950s emboldened Chiang Kai-shek to adopt aggressive and provocative policies, such as raids on mainland China, that risked war. U.S. policymakers at the time feared that the ROC was trying to entangle the United States in the Chinese Civil War.[6] However, without direct evidence about ROC decisionmaking, it is difficult to know whether Chiang's belief that he could retake the mainland and domestic political pressure would have led to such policies even in the absence of a security relationship with the United States.[7]

Another example that scholars sometimes point to is Taiwan's change in foreign policy prior to the 1995–1996 Taiwan Strait Crisis. Taiwanese President Lee Teng-hui's government held meetings with top officials in Southeast Asia, hoping to raise the regional profile of Taiwan and build economic relations.[8] Taiwan also actively sought to join the United Nations General Assembly.[9] Lee's invitation to speak at Cornell University became a watershed moment for U.S.-Taiwanese relations, marking the first visit by a Taiwanese leader to the United States since the normalization of relations between the United States and the PRC. The speech itself solidified trends in Taiwanese foreign policy and proved to be extremely provocative in Beijing. In his speech, Lee promoted the international recognition of Taiwan, referred to Taiwan as "the Republic of China on Taiwan" on multiple occa-

---

[4]   Helene Cooper, C. J. Chivers, and Clifford J. Levy, "U.S. Watched as a Squabble Turned into a Showdown," *New York Times*, August 17, 2008.

[5]   Lanoszka, 2018b.

[6]   Cha, 2016, pp. 70–80.

[7]   For a discussion of Chiang's ambitions and domestic political pressures, see Cha, 2016, p. 70.

[8]   John W. Garver, *Face Off: China, the United States, and Taiwan's Democratization*, Seattle: University of Washington Press, 1997, pp. 27–34.

[9]   Garver, 1997, pp. 31–32.

sions, and did not mention future reunification.[10] Many in the PRC claimed that U.S. support had emboldened Taiwan to take such steps because the preceding time frame had seen increases in the diplomatic and military relations between Taiwan and the United States.[11] Although this is plausible, there has been no conclusive evidence about the extent to which the expectation of U.S. support drove Taiwan to shift its foreign policy before the crisis. Moreover, some scholars claim that domestic political trends in Taiwan led to policies that made a confrontation with China more likely.[12] Researchers have not directly compared these alternative explanations.

These cases highlight the challenges of studying how U.S. security relationships influence the incentives and behaviors of U.S. allies and partners. In these cases, detailed information about state decisionmaking is unavailable, so we are left with circumstantial evidence. Some analysts and policymakers might assess that circumstantial evidence is sufficient in these cases. However, without a systematic review of multiple cases that compare emboldenment with alternative explanations, we do not know how an expectation of U.S. support has generally played into decisions by U.S. allies and partners to engage in conflict. Conversely, even when these states have behaved more cautiously, we do not know whether they have done so because of concerns about damaging their security relationship with the United States, because the U.S. commitment reassured them about their security, or for other reasons.

---

[10] Barton Gellman, "U.S. and China Nearly Came to Blows in '96," *Washington Post*, June 21, 1998; and Robert L. Suettinger, *Beyond Tiananmen: The Politics of U.S.-China Relations 1989–2000*, Washington, D.C.: Brookings Institution Press, 2004.

[11] Garver, 1997, pp. 35–46.

[12] Garver, 1997; Chen Qimao, "The Taiwan Strait Crisis: Its Crux and Solutions," *Asian Survey*, Vol. 36, No. 11, November 1996; and Andrew Scobell, "China and Taiwan: Balance of Rivalry with Weapons of Mass Democratization," *Political Science Quarterly*, Vol. 129, No. 3, Fall 2014.

Do Security Relationships Give the United States Leverage to Restrain Allies and Partners from Initiating or Provoking Conflict?

There is a larger body of literature on U.S. influence once allies and partners are considering embarking on conflict. We focus in this section on historical U.S. cases rather than those involving other countries' alliances and partnerships because there is more research on U.S. cases and because they have many similarities to the dynamics within current U.S. alliances (e.g., asymmetry of power between the United States and its allies and similar alliance terms).[13] Of course, historical U.S. cases also have some differences from U.S. relationships in the contemporary period (e.g., less severe security threats in Europe today than during the Cold War). Still, the literature on U.S. alliances offers the closest available parallels in the literature.

These case studies start from a moment of crisis—when an ally or partner is already considering the use of force. As a result, these studies do not consider whether a state's relationship with the United States may have made the state more or less likely to consider conflict in the first place. These qualitative studies use primary sources on U.S. and allied decisionmaking to analyze how U.S. attempts to restrain allies and partners influenced their decisions.[14]

These studies show that the United States has tried to restrain allies in many cases in the past. At times, U.S. pressure has been key in prevent-

---

[13] For a discussion of non-U.S. cases, see Christensen, 2011. For a discussion of alliance management among states with more-similar levels of power, see Snyder, 1997.

[14] Schroeder, who offers the groundwork for this literature, argues that, historically, "all alliances in some measure functioned as pacts of restraint" (Paul W. Schroeder, "Alliances, 1815–1945: Weapons of Power and Tools of Management," in Klaus Knorr, ed., *Historical Dimensions of National Security*, Lawrence, Kan.: University Press of Kansas, 1976, p. 230). Schroeder provides evidence from the European alliance system from 1815 to 1945 to illustrate how alliances are used for management, control, and restraint in addition to capability aggregation. Weitsman suggests a related concept, *tethering*, in which adversaries ally with one another to try to prevent conflict between themselves (Patricia A. Weitsman, *Dangerous Alliances: Proponents of Peace, Weapons of War*, Stanford, Calif.: Stanford University Press, 2004). Because this is not a form of alliance that the United States has, we do not consider it here.

ing allies from embarking on military interventions. But despite its superior power position and conditional alliance commitments, the United States has not always been able to dissuade allies and partners from using force in ways that run counter to its interests. This does not mean that the United States has always been entangled in such conflicts or unable to exercise alliance restraint after a conflict has already begun.[15] But the literature on alliance restraint offers a window into the claim that United States has leverage over allies, which prevents conflicts more generally, whether the United States becomes involved or not.

These studies point to multiple successful cases of alliance restraint. In 1951, for example, the United States used presidential statements and direct diplomatic contacts to dissuade Britain from a military intervention in Iran.[16] President Truman made clear that the United States would not "consider support of any such action" if Britain chose to act.[17] After several failed attempts to gain U.S. support, the British cabinet ultimately chose not to intervene, privately citing U.S. opposition.[18]

The United States has also successfully restrained South Korea from using force. In 1968, South Korea sought military action against North Korea after it sank a South Korean warship, infiltrated the South with North Korean agents, and attempted to assassinate South Korean leader Park Chung-hee. A U.S. State Department memo delivered to South Korea stressed that "President Johnson urges President Park to be calm and patient, not to permit . . . rash acts which might lead to fighting."[19] An internal memo by U.S. Secretary of State Dean Rusk ahead of a meeting between Park and a U.S. presidential envoy stressed that, if the South Koreans sought to pressure the United States to support an escalatory response by, for example, reducing the number of Korean troops in Vietnam (the primary concern of the Johnson administration at the time), the U.S. diplomat should tell him that the United States would then cut the number of troops in South Korea. In the

---

[15] See our discussion of the First Taiwan Strait Crisis in Chapter Seven.

[16] Pressman, 2008, pp. 45–53.

[17] Pressman, 2008, p. 47.

[18] Pressman, 2008, p. 48.

[19] Kim, 2019, p. 12.

meeting that followed, Park ultimately pledged not to retaliate, averting a larger crisis.[20] Although there is no direct evidence that the U.S. threat led Park to stand down, the timing provides circumstantial evidence to suggest that this is a case of alliance restraint.

While the United States does not have a formal commitment that it can leverage when attempting to restrain its security partners, it does have other tools to induce restraint, such as threats to withhold U.S. military assistance. This appears to have been at work in at least one case. In 1973, Israel was considering a preemptive strike on Egypt and Syria. The United States warned Israel that, if it started a war, it could not count on U.S. aid or arms. This played a significant role in restraining Israel because its leaders feared that, if it provoked the war, Israel would not receive much-needed U.S. assistance.[21] War still broke out in 1973, when a coalition of Arab countries attacked Israel. The United States carried out extensive airlift operations, delivering a continuous flow of materiel to Israel.[22] Although the United States did not prevent the war, it had prevented its partner from launching a preemptive strike.

The literature shows that not all U.S. attempts at restraining allies from entering a conflict have succeeded. In 1956, the United States tried to restrain Britain and France from intervening in Egypt after it nationalized the Suez Canal. Despite clear U.S. opposition, Britain and France, along with Israel, proceeded with war planning in secret and ultimately invaded Egypt. Although U.S. pressure failed at the outset of the conflict, the United States did succeed in influencing its allies as the conflict continued. The United States used economic pressure to compel Britain and France to withdraw from Egypt. Specifically, the United States withheld oil supplies to coerce British and French compliance with a ceasefire. The United States also refused to use its leverage at the International Monetary Fund to shore up the British pound. An analysis of British decisionmaking during the crisis found that U.S. economic pressure was a key reason that Britain even-

---

[20] Kim, 2019, p. 12.

[21] Pressman, 2008, pp. 100–105.

[22] Walter J. Boyne, "Nickel Grass," *Air Force Magazine*, Vol. 81, No. 12, December 1998.

tually agreed to a ceasefire.[23] Although U.S. policy contributed to the de-escalation, we do not consider it to be an example of the logic of alliance restraint. U.S. economic pressure, rather than concerns about the loss of U.S. security commitments, appeared to influence British decisionmaking in this case.[24] This demonstrates how the United States has tools other than its alliance commitments to influence state behavior.

In 1967, the United States repeatedly cautioned its partner Israel against using force after Egypt mobilized forces and closed the Strait of Tiran. Israel did delay an attack when the United States suggested that an international response might be possible. But Israel ultimately decided to attack Egypt despite U.S. objections, starting the Six-Day War.[25]

In 1982, the United States twice failed to restrain Israel from attacking Lebanon. In the first instance, Israel informed the United States of plans for a large-scale invasion of Lebanon in late 1981. The U.S. ambassador to Israel at the time recalled that, for six months, several high-level U.S. officials in the Reagan administration had "urged maximum restraint, cautioned against exaggerating the PLO [Palestine Liberation Organization] military threat, railed against the danger of triggering a major war with Syria, and stressed the broader international implications of unrestrained Israeli military retaliation."[26] Despite these rhetorical warnings, Israel invaded Lebanon, bringing its forces all the way to Beirut. The United States also failed to pressure Israel to negotiate an end to the conflict once it had begun. Israel delayed agreeing to a ceasefire until its forces were able to accomplish certain military objectives in Lebanon. Pressman argues that restraint failed in

---

[23] Pressman, 2008, pp. 68–70.

[24] Beckley and Pressman both consider this incident to be a successful example of alliance restraint, broadly conceived. However, the difference between advocates of restraint and advocates of deep engagement turns on a narrower definition of *alliance restraint*, one that relies on the ability of the United States to threaten to sever its security relationship to gain leverage over an ally. In this case, the authors agree that the cause of Britain's agreement to a ceasefire was economic coercion rather than the threat of security abandonment (Beckley, 2015; Pressman, 2008). For a related argument on the use of economic tools to restrain allies from engaging in nuclear proliferation, see Lanoszka, 2018a.

[25] Pressman, 2008, pp. 91–99.

[26] Pressman, 2008, p. 107.

these two instances because the United States relied on rhetorical opposition alone rather than threatening or imposing materiel costs on Israel and because of a lack of U.S. elite consensus on the issue—then–U.S. Secretary of State Alexander Haig did not fully oppose Israeli military action.[27]

Pressman's analysis, which covered the British and Israeli cases above, asked whether the nature of U.S. policy choices changed the effectiveness of attempts to restrain allies and partners. Pressman found that, in some cases, the United States has sought to only rhetorically dissuade allies or partners from conflicts. In cases in which the United States has taken additional steps, such as threatening to withhold aid during the conflict, it has had more success.[28] We note that Pressman did not find any evidence that the United States ever went so far as to explicitly threaten to end its security relationship with either Britain or Israel.

On net, the existing qualitative literature demonstrates that the United States has been able to restrain some, but not all, of its allies and partners from taking military action in opposition to its preferences. This means that allies and partners have been willing to risk the loss of U.S. support for important interests, did not feel that they required U.S. support to achieve their goals, or did not believe that the United States would abandon them for proceeding despite U.S. objections. Overall, we can say that the U.S. ability and willingness to restrain allies and partners is not universal, even though the United States has significant power advantages.[29]

---

[27] Pressman, 2008, pp. 108–109.

[28] Pressman, 2008.

[29] One quantitative study explored how changes in U.S. troop deployments within a host nation influence the probability that the nation will initiate a military dispute (Carla Martinez Machain and T. Clifton Morgan, "The Effect of US Troop Deployment on Host States' Foreign Policy," *Armed Forces & Society*, Vol. 39, No. 1, January 2013). The study found that higher levels of U.S. troops decrease the likelihood that the host nation will take military action against another state. However, the study did not account for why the U.S. troops are present in the host nation, meaning that, for example, troop deployments that result from security commitments are not treated as distinct from U.S. peacekeeping forces. In addition, the study did not consider country characteristics that could change over time that might make a conflict more or less likely, such as the level of host nation democracy.

Still, more research is needed to answer important policy questions. Because these studies consider only cases in which an ally or partner attempted to alter the status quo, they cannot tell us how often allies and partners have avoided conflict in the first place, how often the United States has sought to restrain allies, or how often the United States has succeeded or failed. Moreover, we do not know much about the conditions under which alliance restraint succeeds or fails.[30] Logically, there might be some security relationships in which the United States has greater leverage and, therefore, a greater ability to restrain its allies and partners.[31] Understanding these differences could help U.S. policymakers identify situations with greater entanglement risks. Finally, it would be helpful to better understand how the leverage associated with U.S. security commitments compares with that of other available tools, such as economic threats.[32] This type of research could help U.S. policymakers predict whether a particular security relationship, conflict type, or other set of conditions would give the United States leverage to restrain an ally or partner from initiating conflict.

How Do Alliance Terms and Dependence Affect State Conflict Behavior Globally?

The preceding sections focused on the literature on U.S. security partnerships. That literature is useful because it speaks directly to the U.S. experience and considers direct evidence about U.S. influence on allies and part-

---

[30] Existing theories about alliance restraint emphasize power advantages as an important predictor of success. However, the cases discussed in this section suggest that power advantages alone are not sufficient. Therefore, in addition to empirical research, scholars need to undertake additional theory development on what leads to successful alliance restraint.

[31] In the next section, we discuss one feature of security relationships that might affect the extent of U.S. leverage: an ally's level of dependence on the United States.

[32] For a discussion of these other tools that the United States might use to influence allies, see Marina E. Henke, *Constructing Allied Cooperation: Diplomacy, Payments, and Power in Multilateral Military Coalitions*, Ithaca, N.Y.: Cornell University Press, 2019a; and Marina E. Henke, "Now That Trump Has Abandoned the Kurds, Will Other Countries Ever Trust the U.S.?" *Washington Post*, October 17, 2019c.

ners. However, one limitation is that it is difficult to know how prevalent these phenomena are and which tend to dominate, since there has not been a comprehensive examination of ally and partner emboldenment, reassurance, or restraint within U.S. security relationships. To provide a more comprehensive sense of how alliances might affect conflict, we also review quantitative research on global trends in alliance and conflict behavior. This literature focuses on formal alliances and how alliance terms and alliance dependence affect a state's propensity to initiate conflicts.[33]

Because the average trends that cross-national quantitative studies uncover might differ from the U.S. experience, it is important to draw conclusions from this literature cautiously. In addition, the initiation of conflict is not a perfect way to measure ally emboldenment and restraint. Behaviors do not necessarily reveal underlying motivations. If a state initiates conflict, it is hard to know whether it did so because the prospect of an ally's support emboldened it or whether there was another motivation. Conversely, when states choose not to initiate conflict, it is difficult to know whether fears of alliance restraint or abandonment were at work. Therefore, this literature cannot distinguish whether an ally's motivations or the U.S. ability to restrain was responsible for the eventual outcome. However, the literature still offers useful evidence about whether states in formal alliances ultimately end up in conflicts at higher or lower rates.

Focusing narrowly on conflict initiation is also an imperfect way to assess emboldenment because the "initiator" in the data set that these studies most frequently use is not always the provocative party. The MID data set makes this explicit by noting that initiation pertains to the first state to take a military action, which is not necessarily the state that is responsible for the dispute or the state that seeks to alter the status quo.[34] This means that quantitative studies will not list a state as the initiator in some instances

---

[33] Specifically, these studies examine MIDs. Songying Fang, Jesse C. Johnson, and Brett Ashley Leeds, "To Concede or to Resist? The Restraining Effect of Military Alliances," *International Organization*, Vol. 68, No. 4, Fall 2014; and Brett Ashley Leeds and Jesse C. Johnson, "Theory, Data, and Deterrence: A Response to Kenwick, Vasquez, and Powers," *Journal of Politics*, Vol. 79, No. 1, January 2017.

[34] Glenn Palmer, Vito D'Orazio, Michael Kenwick, and Matthew Lane, "The MID4 Dataset, 2002–2010: Procedures, Coding Rules and Description," *Conflict Management and Peace Science*, Vol. 32, No. 2, 2015, pp. 238–239.

even if it takes provocative steps that make conflict more likely. Still, it is meaningful to examine the likelihood that a state turns to military instruments even if it does not rule out all provocative behavior.

Alliance Terms

One set of studies asked whether states that join defensive alliances are more likely to initiate or escalate conflict than those with other security relationships (e.g., neutrality pacts, offensive alliances) or no alliances at all.[35] All U.S. alliances are defensive in the sense that they commit the United States to provide military support only in the event of an attack on the ally. Multiple studies have found that, on average, states that have at least one defensive alliance are less likely to initiate conflict than states without a defense alliance.[36] Once a dispute has begun, targeted states with a defensive alliance are less likely to respond with the threat, display, or use of force.[37] In particular, defensive alliances with conditional terms have the strongest association with lower rates of conflict initiation.[38] This suggests that the only type of alliance agreement that the United States has—the conditional defensive alliance—is associated with less conflict. Although these results do not definitively demonstrate that the written terms of alliances are what causes less conflict initiation, they do suggest that there is something common among states with conditional alliance relationships that induces less conflictual behavior.

Other factors, however, such as a state's ambitions, also influence the relationship between alliance commitments and conflict behavior. For example, there is little evidence that even defensive conditional alliances

---

[35] Jesse C. Johnson and Brett Ashley Leeds, "Defense Pacts: A Prescription for Peace?" *Foreign Policy Analysis*, Vol. 7, No. 1, January 2011; Leeds et al., 2002; and U.S. Department of State, undated. According to the U.S. State Department, U.S. collective defense agreements include NATO; the Australia, New Zealand and United States Security Treaty; the Southeast Asia Treaty Organization (SEATO); the Rio Pact; and bilateral agreements with the Philippines, Japan, and the Republic of Korea; these alliances are all listed as defensive in the core data set used in this literature.

[36] Fang, Johnson, and Leeds, 2014; Johnson and Leeds, 2011; Leeds and Johnson, 2017.

[37] Fang, Johnson, and Leeds, 2014; Johnson and Leeds, 2011.

[38] Benson, 2011.

change the behavior of revisionist states—those with publicly stated ambitions for greater territory or status.[39] Revisionist states with conditional defensive alliances still initiate conflict at higher rates than status quo states, and there is no statistically significant difference in the behavior of revisionist states with or without an alliance.[40]

Even for states with more-limited ambitions, there are several things to consider before concluding that defensive alliances either reduce incentives to initiate conflict or help states restrain one another. Because these quantitative studies focus on behavior rather than motivations, other factors beyond alliance considerations could explain the lower rate of conflict initiation. These studies control for many factors that make conflict more likely, such as relative military power, shared democratic institutions, and the distance between the two states. These controls provide a greater degree of confidence that the finding is due to the presence of a defensive alliance, although it is difficult to fully capture a state's decision to initiate a conflict in a quantitative model.

It is also possible that the states that form defensive alliances are systematically different from the states without such alliances. If that is the case, then whatever makes those states different—rather than the alliance itself—might explain the lower rate of conflict initiation. Scholars introduce potential bias into their research by assuming that the existence of a treaty is the only thing that is different between states with and without defensive

---

[39] Brett V. Benson, Patrick R. Bentley, and James Lee Ray, "Ally Provocateur: Why Allies Do Not Always Behave," *Journal of Peace Research*, Vol. 50, No. 1, 2013. Senese and Vasquez, 2008, defines this concept of *revisionism*. States that are not revisionist might still have incentives to initiate conflict in some cases. This group could include those that have not publicly revealed their revisionist intentions as well as status quo states that take preemptive action to defend themselves.

[40] The description of the statistical analysis in Benson, Bentley, and Ray, 2013, suggests that revisionist states might be more likely to initiate a conflict under a conditional defensive alliance than with no alliance. However, using the authors' replication data, we found that the difference in the likelihood of conflict initiation by states in a conditional defensive alliance and by states with no alliance at all is not statistically significant. The results did, however, show that revisionist states in a conditional defensive alliance are less likely to initiate conflict than those with an unconditional defensive agreement.

alliances. Not accounting for these differences—what is known as a *selection effect*—could therefore influence the findings.

There are several pathways through which selection effects could influence findings.[41] In particular, states that become members of defensive alliances might be fundamentally more peaceful countries. This could be the case if states, hoping to avoid entrapment risks, reject reckless or ambitious partners. Leeds and Johnson attempted to account for this possible selection effect by directly comparing states that differ in whether they have a defensive alliance but face a similar risk of conflict based on their characteristics and strategic settings.[42] This methodology, known as *matching*, is a first step toward determining whether alliances restrain or whether it is just that peaceful states tend to form defensive alliances. The authors' results are quite similar to those found without using this methodological approach. However, matching is not a perfect solution. Because it is extremely difficult to find appropriate direct comparisons, the analysis discards some cases, which makes it harder to generalize the results to all states. The more dissimilar the matched comparisons, the greater the risk of bias in the results. Furthermore, this work matches states with similar conflict risks using only observable characteristics. If unobservable characteristics, such as risk propensity, determine the selection of alliance partners and conflict outcomes, matching would not correct for this bias. In addition, this method has not been used to look at more-specific alliance terms, such as conditional commitments.

---

[41] Other selection effects could also occur that would not bias the statistical results in the same fashion. For example, states might choose to offer defensive alliances where they are most needed. That is, the states might offer the alliances where the risk of conflict is particularly high. If this were the case, defensive alliances would be associated with higher conflict overall. Given that the literature shows the opposite, there are two possibilities. One is that a tendency to offer defensive alliances in high-conflict areas does not exist or is small in practice. The other possibility is that the true effect is larger than the literature describes. In either case, the results would still suggest a pacifying or restraining effect of alliances.

[42] Leeds and Johnson, 2017. Morrow finds similar results. James D. Morrow, "When Do Defensive Alliances Provoke Rather Than Deter?" *Journal of Politics*, Vol. 79, No. 1, January 2017.

That said, there is evidence to suggest that this possible selection effect is not that concerning. As we have noted, the United States has been willing to make alliances with revisionist states in the past. Moreover, research on states globally shows that they frequently form defensive alliances with states that have publicly stated ambitions to gain greater territory or status.[43] This cannot entirely exclude the possibility that there are other systematic differences between states with and without defensive alliances, but it does suggest that the extent of potential bias from selecting peaceful allies is likely insufficient to explain these findings. So, we can have greater confidence that there is a real relationship between defensive alliances and less conflict initiation.

On net, the existing evidence is consistent with the argument that defensive conditional alliances either give status quo states fewer reasons for initiating conflict (e.g., because they address security concerns) or help states restrain each other from initiating conflict. However, the existing evidence also suggests that revisionist states will remain just as revisionist if they establish a conditional defensive alliance. Conversely, the findings in this literature are inconsistent with the claim that states in defensive alliances generally initiate more conflicts than they would without such a commitment.

As we noted above, these findings cannot address whether states in defensive alliances become more prone to risk-taking short of conflict. For example, we cannot exclude the possibility that defensive alliances make states more demanding or intransigent in negotiations. What we can say is that that states in defensive alliances do not appear more likely to be the first mover in making military threats, making displays of force, or using force in disputes.

Alliance Dependence

Some strategists claim that allies' dependence on the United States for security gives the United States leverage over them and makes it immune from entrapment. Two factors might make an ally dependent on the United States for security: the level of threat that the ally faces and the significant power advantages that the United States can bring to bear to combat those threats. Unfortunately, there is no existing research on whether external threats

---

[43] Benson, Bentley, and Ray, 2013; Senese and Vasquez, 2008.

affect allied risk-taking.[44] There is a small amount of quantitative literature on alliance power asymmetries and an ally's propensity to initiate conflicts, but the findings in this literature are not conclusive enough to help evaluate claims about alliance dependence in the grand strategy debate.[45]

Some studies that examine the relationship between power, entrapment risk, and alliance restraint have significant methodological problems. For example, Palmer and Morgan did not incorporate key control variables, such as an ally's strength, in their analysis, and there might be important differences between states that have a strong alliance partner and those that do not.[46] Kang claims to have found evidence that states in defensive alliances are more likely to initiate conflict when their alliance partners are strong, but we found that Kang misinterprets the statistical results.[47] Narang and Mehta found that states in a defensive alliance with a nuclear power, a particular form of dependence, are more likely to engage in lim-

---

[44] Related scholarly work has explored the role of external threats in determining the allies that states choose and subsequent alliance cohesion, but scholars have not considered how allied dependence due to threats might affect the risk of entrapment. On alliance formation, see Jesse C. Johnson, "External Threat and Alliance Formation," *International Studies Quarterly*, Vol. 61, No. 3, September 2017. On alliance cohesion, see Evan N. Resnick, "Hang Together or Hang Separately? Evaluating Rival Theories of Wartime Alliance Cohesion," *Security Studies*, Vol. 22, No. 4, 2013.

[45] There is, however, a larger literature discussing the ability of the United States to leverage its power advantage to change allies' behavior in other ways. See, for example, David A. Lake, *Hierarchy in International Relations*, Ithaca, N.Y.: Cornell University Press, 2011.

[46] Glenn Palmer and T. Clifton Morgan, *A Theory of Foreign Policy*, Princeton, N.J.: Princeton University Press, 2011.

[47] Choong-Nam Kang, "Capability Revisited: Ally's Capability and Dispute Initiation," *Conflict Management and Peace Science*, Vol. 34, No. 5, September 2017. Specifically, the author interprets the significance of the interaction term alone rather than the significance of the combined effect of capabilities and alliances. In examining these results using the author's replication files, we found that there is no level of allied military capabilities at which this interactive effect is significant. For an explanation of the appropriate interpretation of interaction terms, see Thomas Brambor, William Roberts Clark, and Matt Golder, "Understanding Interaction Models: Improving Empirical Analyses," *Political Analysis*, Vol. 14, No. 1, Winter 2006; and Bear F. Braumoeller, "Hypothesis Testing and Multiplicative Interaction Terms," *International Organization*, Vol. 58, No. 4, Autumn 2004.

ited forms of conflict than states without such an alliance. However, they did not find that war is more likely between states with nuclear partners and their rivals. The authors argue that this finding indicates that states are more likely to press for—and receive—concessions from their opponents when they have a nuclear ally, thus achieving their ambitions without war. Because the study did not control for an ally's conventional capabilities, it is unclear that having a nuclear ally—as opposed to simply an extremely powerful ally—explains the findings.[48] Disentangling conventional deterrence from the nuclear umbrella is particularly difficult in this case because, as the authors themselves note, these alliances do not necessarily contain an explicit nuclear commitment.

There is one study that provides stronger, more–methodologically sound evidence about the potential effects of an ally's power. It found that, when a state is more dependent on an ally for military support, it is less likely to escalate in response to an adversary's provocation.[49] As with the literature on alliance terms, this study did not fully grapple with the selection effects of how states choose their allies. If strong states choose allies based on characteristics that also affect their likelihood of escalating a dispute, the results might be biased. Still, this study provides preliminary support for the argument that states with a strong ally are less likely to escalate conflicts. If this finding holds up to additional research, it suggests that power advantages might either reassure weaker allies or give the United States leverage to restrain its allies during a crisis.

---

[48] In addition, the authors examined the overall capabilities of the dyad rather than the distribution of power between the states. Neil Narang and Rupal N. Mehta, "The Unforeseen Consequences of Extended Deterrence: Moral Hazard in a Nuclear Client State," *Journal of Conflict Resolution*, Vol. 63, No. 1, 2019.

[49] Fang, Johnson, and Leeds, 2014. This analysis overcomes a difficult methodological hurdle. The authors had to first confront the fact that they had examined only states that had been targeted by an adversary, and the adversary's decision to start a conflict was not random. The authors used a two-stage statistical model in which they first estimated the probability of a state being targeted by a MID and then estimated the state's response.

Summary

There has been little research directly on the question of whether U.S. security relationships embolden allies and partners to adopt policies that make conflict more likely. The literature on alliance restraint is more developed and suggests that the United States has had both successes and failures in preventing its allies and partners from using force in the past. Importantly, there has been little exploration of how the policies that the United States adopts as it manages these relationships (e.g., U.S. force levels within a country) affect the risk of entanglement and the efficacy of alliance restraint.[50]

The existing quantitative literature suggests that states in the type of alliances that the United States has—conditional defensive alliances—are less likely to resort to military tools if a dispute arises. Unfortunately, we know little about how alliance dependence affects conflict behavior. There are several ways in which scholars could develop the quantitative research on alliances and conflict behavior. Most obviously, the literature could consider how partnerships, not just alliances, affect conflict behavior. Qualitative research often draws a distinction between the two, but it is not clear how these relationships might differ.[51] On the one hand, these relationships involve a commitment to come to a partner's defense, which means that, compared with allies, partners might be less likely to be emboldened. On the other hand, given ambiguity about the U.S. commitment, partners might be more prone to making incorrect assumptions about U.S. support. The literature should also consider whether bilateral and multilateral alliances have different effects on allies' conflict behavior.[52] This question is particularly important because some strategists have proposed replacing U.S. bilateral alliances in Asia with a multilateral alliance.[53]

It is worth noting again that this quantitative literature focuses on average effects across alliances globally, not just the U.S. experience, so it is still

---

[50] For the key theoretical examination of alliance management, see Snyder, 1984.

[51] See, for example, Rapp-Hooper, 2020.

[52] Benjamin O. Fordham and Paul Poast, "All Alliances Are Multilateral: Rethinking Alliance Formation," *Journal of Conflict Resolution*, Vol. 60, No. 5, 2016.

[53] See, for example, Mearsheimer and Walt, 2016.

possible that U.S. security relationships might create incentives to engage in risky behavior in individual cases. A current or prospective ally might be particularly prone to risk-taking, and, therefore, additional indications of U.S. support would embolden it in ways that they would not for most allies. It is therefore important to consider the historical record to examine whether, in such cases, the United States is likely to offer its support in conflict.

CHAPTER SEVEN

Does the United States Ultimately Become Entangled in Conflict?

U.S. allies and partners sometimes become involved in conflicts contrary to direct U.S. interests, whether because of emboldenment or for other reasons. In this chapter, we ask whether the United States defends its allies and partners in such situations because of concerns about U.S. credibility. We also consider whether the United States becomes involved in conflict because of other forms of interest expansion, such as socialization with its allies and partners over the course of the relationship. In other words, we ask whether entanglement ultimately occurs in U.S. alliances and partnerships.

One challenge in answering this question is that there is no clear standard for the extent to which alliance considerations must play a role in U.S. decisionmaking for a case to qualify as entanglement. There are usually many factors that affect state decisions about engaging in conflict, especially entering a war.[1] Therefore, demanding that alliance dynamics be the only explanation for U.S. entry to conflict would be setting too high a bar. Rather, in this chapter, we discuss cases in which entanglement contributed to a U.S. decision to enter a conflict. As research in this area continues, it would be helpful to identify not just how often these dynamics take place but also how important they are relative to other factors. The extent to which entanglement plays a role varies in each of the cases that we discuss in this chapter. In every case that we discuss, there are multiple reasons that

---

[1]   For an overview of the various considerations that can affect state choices, see Anika Binnendijk and Miranda Priebe, *An Attack Against Them All? Drivers of Decisions to Contribute to NATO Collective Defense*, Santa Monica, Calif.: RAND Corporation, RR-2964-OSD, 2019.

the United States is engaged in conflict, even though we focus primarily on describing entanglement dynamics. More research is needed to determine how much these dynamics contributed in each individual case.

In the previous chapter, we identified cases in which the United States chose not to enter wars to support allies and partners that initiated conflict despite U.S. objections. For example, the United States did not fight to support Britain and France during the Suez Crisis, in 1956. The United States thought that the intervention was misguided, would harm Western relations with countries in the Middle East and Africa, would undermine U.S. domestic political support for NATO, and would lead to a confrontation with the Soviet Union.[2] Similarly, the United States did not enter the conflict to support Israel in the Six-Day War or Georgia in its 2008 war with Russia. Ashford also notes that the United States chose not to intervene in Rwanda despite allies and partners prompting it to do so.[3]

Beckley's analysis is the most comprehensive analysis of the U.S. experience with entanglement. He examined every interstate conflict the United States engaged in between 1948 and 2010 and asked whether U.S. involvement was due to alliance entanglement. He also included the U.S. partnerships with Israel and Taiwan in the analysis. Beckley argues that direct U.S. interests drove U.S. involvement in most conflicts but finds evidence of entanglement dynamics in five cases: the 1954–1955 and 1995–1996 Taiwan Strait crises, the Vietnam War, and the U.S. interventions in Bosnia and Kosovo. Even in these cases, though, Beckley downplays the importance of entanglement by arguing that direct U.S. interests dominated the decision to intervene. In nine other cases, Beckley finds that entanglement dynamics may have occurred but dismisses them given lower levels of U.S. military involvement. Ultimately, Beckley concludes that entanglement is rare.[4]

---

[2] Although there is no direct evidence, it is possible that the United States had fewer concerns about its reputation in this case because of the geographic limits set forth in the North Atlantic Treaty. Sayle, 2019, pp. 32–33.

[3] The United States also had a lower level of involvement in Syria than its partners in the region preferred. Emma M. Ashford, "Hegemonic Blackmail: Entrapment in Civil War Intervention," *Canadian Foreign Policy Journal*, Vol. 23, No. 3, 2017.

[4] Beckley, 2015, p. 10.

As an illustration, one of Beckley's cases of U.S. entanglement in a conflict short of war is the 1995–1996 Taiwan Strait Crisis. During this period, the PRC undertook extensive exercises and missile tests near Taiwan in response to shifts in Taiwan's foreign policy. As noted in Chapter Six, it is unclear whether U.S. support emboldened Taiwan to take such steps. In either case, Beckley finds that a desire to reassure allies and partners about U.S. commitments and a desire to maintain U.S. credibility with China were central factors in the decision to send two carrier battle groups near Taiwan during the crisis.[5]

Beckley has provided an important contribution to the study of entanglement by compiling a list of cases for scholars to consider and offering a preliminary analysis of many of them. Still, there are a few methodological reasons why Beckley's analysis should not be the final word on the subject.

Beckley conducts only preliminary historical analysis. Because of the large number of conflicts that Beckley considered, he could not examine all cases in detail. Rather, he relied on a limited number of histories of these events to look for evidence of entanglement. More-detailed examinations of ally, partner, and U.S. decisionmaking in each of these conflicts might reveal more cases of entanglement or confirm his current list of cases.

The article does not consider the possibility of entanglement dynamics in some of the most important U.S. alliances. Beckley excludes or downplays the importance of cases of entanglement in which the United States had a national interest at stake.[6] This means that Beckley excludes all cases involving West Germany and South Korea, arguing that the U.S. national interest would have dictated U.S. defense of these countries. Lind, however, discusses government statements from the Berlin Crises and the Korean War in which the United States expressed concerns about allies' perceptions of U.S. reliability.[7] A more detailed examination of conflicts

---

[5] Beckley, 2015, pp. 42–44. Ross makes a similar assessment in this case. Robert S. Ross, "The 1995–96 Taiwan Strait Confrontation: Coercion, Credibility, and the Use of Force," *International Security*, Vol. 25, No. 2, Fall 2000.

[6] Beckley, 2015, p. 25.

[7] Jennifer Lind, "Article Review 52 on 'The Myth of Entangling Alliances.' *International Security* 39:4," International Security Studies Forum, ISSF Article Review 52, April 13, 2016.

involving South Korea and West Germany could clarify the extent to which entanglement dynamics contributed to U.S. choices.

We examined one of these cases—the Korean War—and found evidence that entanglement dynamics contributed to the U.S. decision to fight, even if they were not the only cause.[8] Prior to the North Korean invasion, South Korea was not a U.S. ally, but it was a U.S. partner that received military aid and hosted U.S. military advisers. The United States did not consider South Korea among its top interests, so it had withdrawn its remaining combat forces in 1949 and limited the extent of its military aid to preserve resources for other priorities.[9] When the war began, U.S. decisionmakers believed that the Soviet Union was behind the North Korean attack. Beckley cites U.S. intelligence assessments warning of damage to U.S. credibility with allies if it did not intervene in Korea.[10] Importantly, other scholars have pointed to evidence that such concerns played a critical role in the U.S. decision to intervene. They cite private statements by the President and top administration officials and intelligence and State Department assessments arguing that failing to defend South Korea would dishearten allies as far away as Europe and embolden U.S. adversaries.[11] For example, Secretary of State Dean Acheson argued that reassuring U.S. European allies

---

[8] For Beckley's evidence on this case, see Beckley, 2015, online appendix, pp. 2–5. Kim, 2011, mentions the Korean War as an example in which direct U.S. interests were at stake and dismisses it as a case of entanglement. However, Kim does not provide any evidence or explain the logic behind this assessment.

[9] Cha, 2016, pp. 55–56; Melvyn P. Leffler, *A Preponderance of Power: National Security, the Truman Administration, and the Cold War*, Stanford, Calif.: Stanford University Press, 1992, p. 365; William Stueck, *The Korean War: An International History*, Princeton, N.J.: Princeton University Press, 1995, pp. 16, 25, 29; and William Stueck, *Rethinking the Korean War: A New Diplomatic and Strategic History*, Princeton, N.J.: Princeton University Press, 2002, pp. 78–79.

[10] Beckley, 2015, online appendix, pp. 2–5.

[11] Leffler, 1992, p. 366; Jonathan Mercer, "Emotion and Strategy in the Korean War," *International Organization*, Vol. 67, No. 2, Spring 2013, pp. 232–235. See also Rosemary Foot, *The Wrong War: American Policy and the Dimensions of the Korean Conflict, 1950–1953*, Ithaca, N.Y.: Cornell University Press, 1985, p. 59; Robert J. McMahon, "Credibility and World Power: Exploring the Psychological Dimension in Postwar American Diplomacy," *Diplomatic History*, Vol. 15, No. 4, Fall 1991; and Stueck, 1995, p. 43.

was the most important reason to intervene, explaining, "the governments of many Western European nations appeared to be in a state of near-panic, as they watched to see whether the United States would act or not."[12] Beckley downplays such considerations by arguing that the United States had a direct interest in showing resolve to the Soviet Union,[13] but these two potential causes are not mutually exclusive.

The 1954–1955 Taiwan Strait Crisis offers another example in which Beckley points to direct U.S. interests at stake but credibility concerns appear to have been at work. During 1954, the United States and its partners in the region were in the process of forming SEATO. PRC leaders worried that the United States would turn next toward an alliance treaty with Taiwan, so they began shelling offshore islands that the ROC controlled in an attempt to forestall such a development.[14] For this reason, Beckley considers entanglement dynamics to have partly driven U.S. threats of war during the crisis. Still, he downplays the importance of entanglement dynamics in this case, arguing that the United States had a direct interest in combating the spread of communism to Taiwan.[15]

However, a review of Beckley's sources suggests that entanglement dynamics should not be dismissed as easily as Beckley proposes. Both the Truman and Eisenhower administrations had assessed that the offshore islands were not intrinsically worth defending and were primarily valuable to Taiwan as a base for harassing or conducting offensive operations against the Chinese mainland. During the crisis, U.S. intelligence suggested that there was no threat to Taiwan proper, which the Eisenhower administration said was the actual U.S interest. In other words, defense of the offshore islands was not a direct U.S. interest. Moreover, the United States had never committed to defending the offshore islands prior to the crisis.[16]

---

[12] Mercer, 2013, p. 234.

[13] Beckley, 2015.

[14] Christensen, 2011, pp. 136–139.

[15] Beckley, 2015, also notes the possibility that the United States had an interest in showing its willingness to use nuclear weapons, a centerpiece of the administration's New Look defense program. See also Christensen, 2011.

[16] H. W. Brands, Jr., "Testing Massive Retaliation: Credibility and Crisis Management in the Taiwan Strait," *International Security*, Vol. 12, No. 4, Spring 1988; and Gordon H.

During the crisis, the United States offered Taiwan the mutual defense treaty (discussed in Chapter Five) that it had long wanted in exchange for Taiwan's agreement to accept United Nations mediation of the crisis.[17] As the crisis escalated, the United States pressured Taiwan to accept and assisted with the evacuation of ROC forces from the Tachen Islands, the off-shore islands closest to mainland China. U.S. naval forces had the authority to fire on the Chinese mainland if U.S. forces were attacked during the withdrawal, but, fortunately, the evacuation was uncontested.[18] During the crisis, the United States succeeded in limiting further escalation over the defense of the Tachen Islands through this policy. However, President Eisenhower sought unsuccessfully to convince the ROC to treat some of the remaining offshore islands as expendable.[19] When Taiwan refused, U.S. leaders believed that an intervention might be necessary to defend them. The logic was that the U.S. partnership with Taiwan meant that U.S. credibility was on the line with Taiwan, other U.S. partners, China, and the Soviet Union if the United States failed to intervene. The U.S. interest in preventing communism on the main island of Taiwan had expanded to the defense of offshore islands that Eisenhower assessed were not strictly required for the security of Taiwan.[20] This was the case even though the administration expected that intervention would lead to a war with China and possibly the Soviet Union, involve the use of nuclear weapons, and harm relations between the United States and its European allies. Fortunately, the PRC offered to negotiate an end to the crisis.[21] Beckley argues that the United States would not have gone to

---

Chang, "To the Nuclear Brink: Eisenhower, Dulles, and the Quemoy-Matsu Crisis," *International Security*, Vol. 12, No. 4, Spring 1988.

[17] Brands, 1988, pp. 131–134.

[18] Brands, 1988, p. 141.

[19] Brands, 1988, p. 144–146.

[20] Robert Accinelli, "Eisenhower, Congress, and the 1954–55 Offshore Island Crisis," *Presidential Studies Quarterly*, Vol. 20, No. 2, Spring 1990, p. 341; Robert Accinelli, *Crisis and Commitment: United States Policy Toward Taiwan, 1950–1955*, Chapel Hill, N.C.: The University of North Carolina Press, 1996, pp. 190, 193; Brands, 1988; Chang, 1988; and Henry, 2020, pp. 62–72.

[21] Accinelli, 1990, p. 341; Accinelli, 1996, pp. 190, 193; Brands, 1988; McMahon, 1991, pp. 461–465. For a discussion of European pressure not to escalate the crisis, see Henry,

war if it came to it. Regardless, the case follows the logic of entanglement in that, to protect U.S. credibility, the United States made threats of war and seriously considered a military intervention—which the administration expected would involve the use of nuclear weapons—to protect islands of no intrinsic value to the United States.

Beckley's research design did not allow him to evaluate all forms of interest expansion. Beckley asks whether the United States saw its interests as being directly at stake at the time of the crisis. If so, he contends, then entanglement did not take place.[22] However, this approach does not test the claim made by advocates of restraint that the way in which the United States defines its interests grows as the result of security relationships and, potentially, before a crisis even takes place. From this perspective, evidence that the United States saw an intervention as being in its own interest during a crisis is not sufficient to exclude this form of entanglement.[23]

Beckley's standard for what constitutes a concerning level of entanglement is contested. Other scholars have raised concerns about Beckley's conclusion that U.S. policymakers should not worry too much about the risk of entanglement. They note that Beckley does not establish a clear standard for what a concerning number of cases of entanglement would be. Even if the number of cases is ultimately small, they argue, the cases that Beckley counts as entanglement, including the Vietnam War, were consequential for the United States.[24]

Although the methodological issues above mean that there might be cases of entanglement that Beckley missed or that are more meaningful than he allows, there are also cases in which the evidence that he presents is not decisive. This is because Beckley asks whether alliance considerations affected U.S. decisionmaking in each case but does not provide evidence that alliance considerations constituted entanglement. For example, Beckley notes that, after NATO made threats against Serbia for its actions in

---

2020, p. 64.

[22] Beckley, 2015, p. 10.

[23] Lind, 2016, makes a similar critique.

[24] Daniel W. Drezner, "Just How Entangling Are America's Alliances?" *Washington Post*, August 4, 2015; and Lind, 2016.

Kosovo in 1998, the United States felt that NATO credibility was on the line. When Serbia did not meet NATO demands, the United States felt that NATO had to intervene. This is certainly an alliance consideration. However, Beckley does not show what made U.S. leaders put NATO credibility at stake by issuing the threat in the first place. Other analysis suggests that U.S. humanitarian concerns motivated the United States to seek NATO involvement and that allies tried to restrain the United States from using force earlier in the crisis.[25]

Similar questions surround the U.S. intervention in Bosnia in the 1990s. The Clinton administration had said that it would intervene to protect NATO allies with peacekeepers in Bosnia, which Beckley argues was intended to keep these allies from pulling their forces. When these peacekeepers were seriously threatened in 1995, the administration intervened in part to help its allies and because it saw NATO credibility as being on the line.[26] However, Beckley does not explain why the United States believed that NATO's credibility was at stake, why the United States promoted air strikes as early as 1993, or why the United States had become involved in military operations related to Bosnia, such as Operation Deny Flight, prior to 1995.[27] Ultimately, more evidence is necessary to show that entanglement drove U.S. involvement in the wars in Bosnia and Kosovo. For example, future analysis could consider the possibility that this and the earlier intervention in Bosnia might be a case of interest expansion, in which the United States came to see any instability in Europe as a threat to U.S. allies.[28] In

---

[25] Stefano Recchia, *Reassuring the Reluctant Warriors: U.S. Civil-Military Relations and Multilateral Intervention*, Ithaca, N.Y.: Cornell University Press, 2015.

[26] Beckley, 2015, p. 40; and Steven L. Burg and Paul S. Shoup, *The War in Bosnia-Herzegovina: Ethnic Conflict and International Intervention*, Armonk, N.Y.: M. E. Sharpe, 1999, p. 323.

[27] For a brief overview of U.S. operations prior to 1995, see Karl Mueller, "The Demise of Yugoslavia and the Destruction of Bosnia: Strategic Causes, Effects, and Responses," in Robert C. Owen, ed., *Deliberate Force: A Case Study in Effective Air Campaigning*, Maxwell Air Force Base, Ala.: Air University Press, January 2000. On earlier U.S. proposals for air strikes, see Burg and Shoup, 1999, pp. 251–254. Burg and Shoup also emphasize the domestic political incentives facing President Clinton.

[28] On this possibility, see Layne, 2007, p. 130.

both cases, more in-depth analysis will be possible as government documents from this period are declassified.

In the case of U.S. involvement in Vietnam (1954–1973), Beckley says that alliance credibility concerns contributed to the U.S. intervention but does not provide any direct evidence. Instead, his discussion of Vietnam focuses on dismissing arguments from other scholars about possible entanglement dynamics.[29] So, it is not clear exactly how Beckley believes alliance dynamics affected U.S. decisionmaking or why he says that this qualifies as a case of entanglement. As a result, we reviewed several sources to clarify when and how credibility concerns played a role in U.S. decisionmaking.

U.S. presidents from Truman to Nixon made choices about the level of U.S. involvement in Vietnam. Given the focus of this report—the initial choice to enter a conflict—the Kennedy administration's decision to allow U.S. forces to take part in combat operations in Vietnam is the most relevant.[30] Presidents Truman and Eisenhower both believed that preventing the spread of communism in Southeast Asia was a direct U.S. interest given the raw materials in the region and that, if Vietnam fell to communism, the entire region would fall.[31] Decisionmakers in the Truman administration also voiced concerns that a French loss in Vietnam would make

[29] Beckley, 2015, pp. 36–38.

[30] Kennedy significantly increased the number of U.S. military personnel in Vietnam and also moved beyond just a training and advisory mission by allowing some of them to become involved in combat by, for example, airlifting South Vietnamese combat forces. For the components of the administration's policy for deeper U.S. military involvement in Vietnam, see McGeorge Bundy, "First Phase of Viet-Nam Program," National Security Action Memorandum No. 111, memorandum to the Secretary of State, November 22, 1961, in Ronald D. Landa and Charles S. Sampson, eds., *Foreign Relations of the United States, 1961–1963*: Vol. I, *Vietnam, 1961*, Washington, D.C.: U.S. Government Printing Office, 1988, Document 272. For context on this document, see David Kaiser, *American Tragedy: Kennedy, Johnson, and the Origins of the Vietnam War*, Cambridge, Mass.: Harvard University Press, 2000, pp. 114–123; and Fredrik Logevall, *Choosing War: The Lost Chance for Peace and the Escalation of War in Vietnam*, Berkeley, Calif.: University of California Press, 1999, p. 33.

[31] For a discussion of the nature of this type of domino theory logic in these administrations, see Jerome Slater, "The Domino Theory and International Politics: The Case of Vietnam," *Security Studies*, Vol. 3, No. 2, 1993.

France, a key U.S. ally, more vulnerable to communist influence.[32] Both administrations provided military and economic support to keep France and South Vietnamese forces in the fight and to avoid a U.S. military intervention.[33] Over the course of the Eisenhower administration, the United States increased its involvement by, for example, undertaking covert sabotage activities in the north and allowing U.S. military trainers to provide advice during combat missions. It also considered a military intervention at that time but did not win congressional support.[34] Importantly, when negotiating the Manila Pact that created SEATO, the Eisenhower administration ensured that Vietnam, along with Laos and Cambodia, would be covered by the treaty's defense commitments (even though these countries were prohibited from joining SEATO as members because of the provisions of the 1954 Geneva Agreements).[35] These early decisions established a U.S. partnership with South Vietnam that would set the stage for the decision to have U.S. forces engage in combat during the Kennedy administration.[36]

Concerns about U.S. credibility affected U.S. decisions to increase direct military involvement in Vietnam as early as 1961.[37] A 1961 memorandum arguing for deeper U.S. involvement in Vietnam from the secretaries of the State Department and the Defense Department to President Kennedy is the

---

[32] Fredrik Logevall, *Embers of War: The Fall of an Empire and the Making of America's Vietnam*, New York: Random House, 2012, pp. 186, 231.

[33] Beckley, 2015, pp. 36–38; Leffler, 1992, pp. 434–436, 469, 472; Logevall, 2012, pp. 184, 224, 312, 319, 339, 427; and Office of Joint History, Office of the Chairman of the Joint Chiefs of Staff, *The Joint Chiefs of Staff and the First Indochina War, 1947–1954*, Washington, D.C.: Joint Chiefs of Staff, 2004. These sources also point to concerns about the region's role in the economic recovery of Japan and domestic political pressure to take a stand against communism. For a discussion on implications for Japan, see Leffler, 1992, pp. 434, 470; Logevall, 2012, p. 221.

[34] Logevall, 2012, pp. 634–635, 698.

[35] Yuen Foong Khong, *Analogies at War: Korea, Munich, Dien Bien Phu, and the Vietnam Decisions of 1965*, Princeton, N.J.: Princeton University Press, 1992, p. 80.

[36] For an overview of U.S. policy across administrations, see Fredrik Logevall, "The Indochina Wars and the Cold War, 1945–1975," in Melvyn P. Leffler and Odd Arne Westad, eds., *The Cambridge History of the Cold War*: Volume II, *Crises and Détente*, Cambridge, UK: Cambridge University Press, 2010.

[37] Logevall, 1999, p. 31; Slater, 1993, p. 191.

key piece of evidence that historians point to when making this claim. In addition to making arguments about the danger of communism spreading further if South Vietnam fell and raising domestic political considerations, this memo argued that the "the loss of South Viet-Nam to Communism would not only destroy SEATO but would undermine the credibility of American commitments elsewhere."[38] Historians have also argued that credibility concerns were present in the Johnson administration's decisions to escalate substantially and in later decisions about whether and how to withdraw from Vietnam.[39] Although historians have examined the case of the Vietnam War at length, a more in-depth analysis of U.S. decision-making about Vietnam with questions of entanglement in mind could help identify the extent to which they drove U.S. decisions to intervene militarily throughout this period compared with other factors. For now, we can say that the available evidence suggests that entanglement dynamics played some role in U.S. decisions to become directly militarily involved in Vietnam in the Kennedy and Johnson administrations.

There is also evidence of entanglement in cases beyond the scope of Beckley's analysis, such as the 2011 U.S. intervention in Libya.[40] At the time, U.S. officials made statements about direct U.S. interests in upholding regional stability in the wake of the Arab Spring and protecting human rights.[41] In a Senate resolution calling for the enforcement of a no-fly zone, U.S. lawmak-

---

[38] "1961 Rusk-McNamara Report to Kennedy on South Vietnam," *New York Times*, July 1, 1971. Logevall is not explicit about which evidence supports his claim that credibility concerns emerged in 1961, but Slater specifically points to the Rusk-McNamara memo.

[39] Allan Dafoe and Devin Caughey, "Honor and War: Southern US Presidents and the Effects of Concern for Reputation," *World Politics*, Vol. 68, No. 2, April 2016, pp. 356–357; and McMahon, 1991, p. 46. Logevall notes that the President's fear of personal humiliation and domestic political pressure were additional considerations beyond international credibility concerns; Logevall, 1999, pp. 289, 388–393. On these dynamics in the Nixon administration, see, for example, Johannes Kadura, *The War After the War: The Struggle for Credibility During America's Exit from Vietnam*, Ithaca, N.Y.: Cornell University Press, 2016, pp. 26–28; and Henry A. Kissinger, "The Viet Nam Negotiations," *Foreign Affairs*, Vol. 47, No. 2, January 1969.

[40] Beckley's analysis covered the period up to 2010.

[41] Kevin Marsh, "'Leading from Behind': Neoclassical Realism and Operation Odyssey Dawn," *Defense & Security Analysis*, Vol. 30, No. 2, 2014; and Joshua Miller, "Defense

ers also emphasized human rights concerns.[42] However, in explaining their motivations for intervening to the American public in the days after combat operations commenced, both Secretary of Defense Robert Gates and Secretary of State Hillary Clinton said that pressure from U.S. allies and partners contributed to the decision to intervene. As Clinton put it, "[H]ow could you stand by when, you know, France and the United Kingdom and other Europeans and the Arab League and your Arab partners were saying you've got to do something[?]"[43]

Ashford documents the French and British lobbying campaign to sway the United States and cites statements by Gates and President Obama in the years that followed that suggest that pressure from Britain, France, and other partners contributed to the U.S. decision to intervene.[44] It is difficult to assess the extent to which such public justifications and statements after the fact reflect internal deliberations at the time. But to the extent that they do, they suggest that solidarity with allies and partners—not just direct interests at stake—affected U.S. decisionmaking. Unlike in the earlier Taiwan cases, the United States directly participated in combat operations, firing 112 cruise missiles in the first major attack of the war's international component.[45] More information on the administration's internal deliberations might come out as time passes, which will allow a better sense of the importance of pressure from allies and partners relative to U.S. humanitarian and regional stability concerns. For now, the available evidence suggests that entanglement dynamics contributed to, but were not the only consideration in, the U.S. intervention in Libya.

Taking these considerations into account, the existing literature suggests that entanglement dynamics have contributed to U.S. involvement in con-

---

Secretary: Libya Did Not Pose Threat to U.S., Was Not 'Vital National Interest' to Intervene," ABC News, March 27, 2011.

[42] U.S. Senate, A Resolution Strongly Condemning the Gross and Systematic Violations of Human Rights in Libya, Including Violent Attacks on Protesters Demanding Democratic Reforms, and for Other Purposes, Bill 85, March 1, 2011.

[43] Miller, 2011.

[44] Ashford, 2017.

[45] Jeremiah Gertler, *Operation Odyssey Dawn (Libya): Background and Issues for Congress*, Washington, D.C.: Congressional Research Service, R41725, March 30, 2011.

flict in the past. In at least five cases—the Korean War, the Vietnam War, the Taiwan Strait crises of 1954–1955 and 1995–1996, and the U.S. intervention in Libya in 2011—there is evidence that entanglement dynamics played a role. This evidence comes from political scientists focused on entrapment and historians who have studied the Taiwan cases. In several other cases, scholars have argued that entanglement was at work alongside additional causes. Deeper analyses of these cases would help clarify the prevalence and importance of entanglement dynamics in U.S. alliances relative to other factors.

Beckley's examination suggests that there are no obvious cases of U.S. entrapment in war. Importantly, neither advocates of restraint nor other scholars of alliance politics have suggested a case that fits these criteria either.[46] Because the number of U.S. wars is limited and wars are better studied than conflicts short of war, the negative finding seems like reasonable evidence that entrapment is not common and perhaps has never happened.

The research done thus far represents a starting point for future work on these questions. Going forward, scholars should assess the prevalence of U.S. entrapment in conflicts short of war and consider the entanglement risks associated with U.S. partnerships and formal alliances. Because the existing literature examines only cases of U.S. involvement in conflict, it would also be helpful to analyze cases in which the United States ultimately did not intervene despite allies seeking its involvement. There is a growing amount of literature on the conditions under which policymakers feel they must fight for reputation.[47] As this literature grows, we might be able to better understand situations that increase the risk of entanglement.

---

[46] Kim, 2011.

[47] For an overview of this literature, see Robert Jervis, Keren Yarhi-Milo, and Don Casler, "Redefining the Debate over Reputation and Credibility in International Security: Promises and Limits of New Scholarship," *World Politics*, Vol. 73, No. 1, January 2021. In the past, scholars have often focused on the question of whether fighting to defend U.S. credibility is really necessary to deter adversaries and reassure allies and partners. See, for example, Daryl G. Press, *Calculating Credibility: How Leaders Assess Military Threats*, Ithaca, N.Y.: Cornell University Press, 2005; and Alex Weisiger and Keren Yarhi-Milo, "Revisiting Reputation: How Past Actions Matter in International Politics," *International Organization*, Vol. 69, No. 2, Spring 2015.

The existing literature on entanglement has focused largely on the role of credibility with allies and partners leading to potential entanglement. One particularly underdeveloped area is the possibility of socialization leading to U.S. interest expansion and subsequent involvement in conflict. Cooley and Nexon argue that officials in the administration of President George W. Bush built strong personal friendships with the ruling elites in Georgia and that Georgia engaged in significant lobbying to build ties with lawmakers across the aisle.[48] These policymakers became invested in the success and survival of Georgia and the regime of Georgian leader Mikheil Saakashvili. As a result, Georgia elicited economic, military, and political support; received aid packages; held high-visibility meetings; and enhanced military training and security cooperation. The Bush administration also made efforts to secure a NATO membership action plan for Georgia.[49] Although these ties did not lead to U.S. involvement in the 2008 Russia-Georgia War, the possibility that socialization occurred in this case suggests the value of asking whether it has been at work in cases in which the United States did intervene on behalf of a partner.[50]

Just as the United States might seek to restrain its partners and allies from engaging in behavior counter to its interests, some analysts have suggested that U.S. partners and allies might be able to restrain the United States, reducing the occurrence of entrapment. While researchers have analyzed how U.S. allies attempt to restrain U.S. foreign policy in general, they have not done so in the context of allied efforts to restrain the United States from becoming entangled in a conflict by another state. This research has found some examples of successful restraint of the United States. In the 1958 Berlin Crisis, for example, the United States took a much more bellicose position than its allies. Both the French and the British refused to commit to the use of force to maintain land access to Berlin, and the British refused any ground mobilization without the consensus of all NATO members.[51] Although the United States did not become as moderate as its allies, pres-

---

[48] Cooley and Nexon, 2016.

[49] Cooley and Nexon, 2016.

[50] Cooley and Nexon, 2016.

[51] Press, 2005, p. 107.

sure from its allies led the United States to act more cautiously.[52] Beckley notes that the Clinton administration initially abstained from initiating air strikes in Bosnia because of pressure from France and Britain.[53]

However, allies and partners have not always succeeded in restraining the United States. For example, France failed to restrain the United States from invading Iraq in 2003.[54] During the Vietnam War, the United States resisted pressure from its European allies to reduce its involvement.[55] During the First Taiwan Strait Crisis, from 1954 to 1955, Britain, New Zealand, and other U.S. allies worked to restrain the scope of the U.S. response, although the United States continued planning for conflict despite these objections.[56] There might be successful cases of ally restraint of the United States that have not yet been considered. However, the available evidence suggests that the diversity of U.S. alliances alone is not always a check on entanglement.

---

[52] Trachtenberg, 1999.

[53] Beckley, 2015, p. 39.

[54] Pressman, 2008, p. 1.

[55] Beckley, 2015, pp. 32–34; and Eugenie M. Blang, *Allies at Odds: America, Europe, and Vietnam, 1961–1968*, Lanham, Md.: Rowman & Littlefield Publishers, Inc., 2011.

[56] Henry, 2020; Brands, 1988.

CHAPTER EIGHT

Findings and Conclusion

Key Findings

Although more research is needed on the U.S. experience of entanglement, there are some useful findings that we can offer U.S. policymakers based on the existing literature.

In at Least Five Cases, Entanglement Dynamics Contributed to, but Were Not the Only Cause of, U.S. Involvement in Conflict; More Research Is Needed on How Prevalent and Consequential These Dynamics Are

The existing literature shows that the United States became involved in two crises over Taiwan at least in part because of concerns about U.S. credibility being on the line. Concerns about U.S. credibility with allies, partners, and adversaries appear to have contributed to U.S. involvement in these cases as well as in the Korean War and Vietnam War. The U.S. intervention in Libya also displays entanglement dynamics because the United States supported its allies in a conflict despite the lack of a vital U.S. interest at stake. In each case, entanglement dynamics contributed to but were not the only cause of a U.S. intervention. Scholars have suggested several other potential cases of entanglement dynamics at work, including U.S. involvement in the wars in Bosnia and Kosovo. However, more in-depth analysis of these cases is needed to make a definitive conclusion about the role of entanglement dynamics.

At the same time, entanglement does not occur in every case of conflict involving U.S. allies and partners. The United States has chosen, in some cases, such as the Suez Crisis, not to support its allies and partners that become involved in conflicts contrary to U.S. interests. This mixed picture suggests that more research is needed on U.S. entanglement dynamics to determine how prevalent and consequential they are and when they are most likely to take place. For some analysts, the small number of known cases of entanglement dynamics across the history of U.S. security relationships suggests that entanglement concerns should not weigh heavily in decisions about U.S. alliance and partnership choices going forward. For others, even a small number of consequential examples is troubling. Ultimately, policymakers and the public have to make a normative choice about how to weigh these risks against other costs and benefits of U.S. alliances and partnerships. More empirical work on entanglement will provide a stronger basis for these assessments.

The United States Has Attempted to Restrain Allies and Partners from Initiating Conflict in the Past, with Both Successes and Failures

Advocates of U.S. military involvement abroad argue that alliances and partnerships give the United States leverage to restrain other states from using force. However, the existing literature suggests that, while the United States has restrained the risky behavior of its allies and partners in some instances, in others, the United States has sought unsuccessfully to rein in its allies and partners. It is not clear whether this is because the United States did not have sufficient leverage or because it preferred not to exercise that leverage.

Scholars Have Not Identified Any Cases of U.S. Entrapment in War

While there is evidence of the broader phenomenon of entanglement, we find no cases in which the United States fought a war to defend an ally that the U.S. commitment emboldened to risk conflict. The frequency of entrapment in conflict short of war is a question that requires further research. Although some participants in the grand strategy debate point to the risk of entrapment, we find that other forms of entanglement deserve greater attention.

The United States Has Allied with Ambitious States in the Past, But It Sought to Minimize Entanglement Risks Through Conditional Alliance Terms

U.S. leaders have, at least twice, formed an alliance with a country that they believed presented an elevated risk of entrapment. In these cases, the United States sought to reduce the risk of entrapment by placing conditions on when it would come to the ally's defense. It is unclear whether these terms have helped the United States reduce entanglement risks as U.S. leaders hoped.

Globally, Alliance Commitments Do Not Lead Most Allies to Adopt Policies That Risk Conflict, But U.S. Alliances Could Still Lead Individual States to Adopt Such Policies

Scholars have not focused on the question of whether U.S. alliances embolden allies and partners to adopt policies that risk conflict. However, the wider literature on alliances globally suggests that states in conditional defensive alliances, the only type of alliance the United States has, are less likely to take initial military action in a dispute than states with no alliances or other types of alliances. This finding suggests that states in such alliances are less likely to consider conflict in the first place or that their partners restrain them when they do. Still, considering the existing literature, we cannot exclude the possibility that the protection that the United States offers might cause individual allies and partners to be more likely to risk conflict.

Conclusion

We do not make recommendations in this report about whether the United States should expand or downsize its network of alliances and partnerships. Such choices depend on a larger set of considerations, beyond entanglement risks. We do, however, recommend that policymakers take these risks into account. There is evidence that the United States has been entangled in conflicts relating to Taiwan in the past, and there is preliminary evidence of U.S. entanglement in wars. These examples suggest that the consequences of entanglement are potentially significant and highlight the importance of continued research on entanglement to inform strategic choices in the years ahead. Although questions about past U.S. entanglement remain, we know that the likelihood of future entanglement is not predetermined. U.S. policymakers ultimately have a choice about how much to incorporate ally and partner interests into the definition of U.S. interests, how far to go to restrain U.S. allies and partners, and when to fight to support an ally or partner.

Abbreviations

MID	militarized interstate dispute
NATO	North Atlantic Treaty Organization
PRC	People's Republic of China
ROC	Republic of China
SEATO	Southeast Asia Treaty Organization

References

"1961 Rusk-McNamara Report to Kennedy on South Vietnam," *New York Times*, July 1, 1971. As of June 21, 2021:
https://www.nytimes.com/1971/07/01/archives/
1961-ruskmcnamara-report-to-kennedy-on-south-vietnam.html

Accinelli, Robert, "Eisenhower, Congress, and the 1954–55 Offshore Island Crisis," *Presidential Studies Quarterly*, Vol. 20, No. 2, Spring 1990, pp. 329–348.

———, *Crisis and Commitment: United States Policy Toward Taiwan, 1950–1955*, Chapel Hill, N.C.: The University of North Carolina Press, 1996.

Art, Robert J., *A Grand Strategy for America*, Ithaca, N.Y.: Cornell University Press, 2003.

———, "Selective Engagement in the Era of Austerity," in Richard Fontaine and Kristin M. Lord, eds., *America's Path: Grand Strategy for the Next Administration*, Washington, D.C.: Center for a New American Security, May 2012, pp. 13–28.

Ashford, Emma M., "Hegemonic Blackmail: Entrapment in Civil War Intervention," *Canadian Foreign Policy Journal*, Vol. 23, No. 3, 2017, pp. 218–231.

———, "Power and Pragmatism: Reforming American Foreign Policy for the 21st Century," in Richard Fontaine and Loren DeJonge Schulman, eds., *New Voices in Grand Strategy*, Washington, D.C.: Center for a New American Security, 2019, pp. 3–12.

Bandow, Doug, "The U.S. Doesn't Need the Philippines," *New York Times*, updated October 18, 2016.

Beckley, Michael, "The Myth of Entangling Alliances: Reassessing the Security Risks of U.S. Defense Pacts," *International Security*, Vol. 39, No. 4, Spring 2015, pp. 7–48.

Benson, Brett V., "Unpacking Alliances: Deterrent and Compellent Alliances and Their Relationship with Conflict, 1816–2000," *Journal of Politics*, Vol. 73, No. 4, October 2011, pp. 1111–1127.

Benson, Brett V., Patrick R. Bentley, and James Lee Ray, "Ally Provocateur: Why Allies Do Not Always Behave," *Journal of Peace Research*, Vol. 50, No. 1, 2013, pp. 47–58.

Berger, Miriam, "The U.S. Relationship with Ukraine Runs Deep. Here's Why," *Washington Post*, November 12, 2019.

Bergman, Ronen, and Mark Mazzetti, "The Secret History of the Push to Strike Iran," *New York Times*, last updated May 23, 2021.

Biden, Joseph R., Jr., "Why America Must Lead Again: Rescuing U.S. Foreign Policy After Trump," *Foreign Affairs*, Vol. 99, No. 2, March–April 2020, pp. 64–76.

Binnendijk, Anika, and Miranda Priebe, *An Attack Against Them All? Drivers of Decisions to Contribute to NATO Collective Defense*, Santa Monica, Calif.: RAND Corporation, RR-2964-OSD, 2019. As of July 29, 2021: https://www.rand.org/pubs/research_reports/RR2964.html

Blang, Eugenie M., *Allies at Odds: America, Europe, and Vietnam, 1961–1968*, Lanham, Md.: Rowman & Littlefield Publishers, Inc., 2011.

Bleek, Philipp C., and Eric B. Lorber, "Security Guarantees and Allied Nuclear Proliferation," *Journal of Conflict Resolution*, Vol. 58, No. 3, April 2014, pp. 429–454.

Boyne, Walter J., "Nickel Grass," *Air Force Magazine*, Vol. 81, No. 12, December 1998, pp. 54–59.

Brambor, Thomas, William Roberts Clark, and Matt Golder, "Understanding Interaction Models: Improving Empirical Analyses," *Political Analysis*, Vol. 14, No. 1, Winter 2006, pp. 63–82.

Brands, H. W., Jr., "Testing Massive Retaliation: Credibility and Crisis Management in the Taiwan Strait," *International Security*, Vol. 12, No. 4, Spring 1988, pp. 124–151.

Brands, Hal, "Fools Rush Out? The Flawed Logic of Offshore Balancing," *Washington Quarterly*, Vol. 38, No. 2, 2015a, pp. 7–28.

———, "Rethinking America's Grand Strategy: Insights from the Cold War," *Parameters*, Vol. 45, No. 4, Winter 2015b, pp. 7–16.

———, "Choosing Primacy: U.S. Strategy and Global Order at the Dawn of the Post–Cold War Era," *Texas National Security Review*, Vol. 1, No. 2, February 2018, pp. 8–33.

Brands, Hal, and Peter Feaver, "Should America Retrench? The Battle over Offshore Balancing: The Risks of Retreat," *Foreign Affairs*, Vol. 95, No. 6, November–December 2016, pp. 164–169.

———, "What Are America's Alliances Good For?" *Parameters*, Vol. 47, No. 2, Summer 2017, pp. 15–30.

Braumoeller, Bear F., "Hypothesis Testing and Multiplicative Interaction Terms," *International Organization*, Vol. 58, No. 4, Autumn 2004, pp. 807–820.

Brooks, Stephen G., G. John Ikenberry, and William C. Wohlforth, "Don't Come Home, America: The Case Against Retrenchment," *International Security*, Vol. 37, No. 3, Winter 2012–2013, pp. 7–51.

———, "Lean Forward: In Defense of American Engagement," *Foreign Affairs*, Vol. 92, No. 1, January–February 2013, pp. 130–142.

Brooks, Stephen G., and William C. Wohlforth, *America Abroad: The United States' Global Role in the 21st Century*, New York: Oxford University Press, 2016.

Bundy, McGeorge, "First Phase of Viet-Nam Program," National Security Action Memorandum No. 111, memorandum to the Secretary of State, November 22, 1961, in Ronald D. Landa and Charles S. Sampson, eds., *Foreign Relations of the United States, 1961–1963:* Vol. I, *Vietnam, 1961*, Washington, D.C.: U.S. Government Printing Office, 1988, Document 272. As of August 11, 2021:
https://history.state.gov/historicaldocuments/frus1961-63v01/d272

Bureau of Near Eastern Affairs, "U.S. Relations with Morocco," fact sheet, U.S. Department of State, November 5, 2020. As of September 29, 2021:
https://www.state.gov/u-s-relations-with-morocco/

———, "U.S. Relations with Israel," fact sheet, U.S. Department of State, January 20, 2021. As of September 29, 2021:
https://www.state.gov/u-s-relations-with-israel/

Bureau of Political-Military Affairs, "Major Non-NATO Ally Status," fact sheet, U.S. Department of State, January 20, 2021. As of June 25, 2021:
https://www.state.gov/major-non-nato-ally-status/

Burg, Steven L., and Paul S. Shoup, *The War in Bosnia-Herzegovina: Ethnic Conflict and International Intervention*, Armonk, N.Y.: M. E. Sharpe, 1999.

Carpenter, Ted Galen, *America's Coming War with China: A Collision Course over Taiwan*, New York: Palgrave MacMillan, 2005.

———, "It's Time to Suspend America's Alliance with the Philippines," *National Interest*, October 1, 2016.

Cha, Victor D., "Powerplay: Origins of the U.S. Alliance System in Asia," *International Security*, Vol. 34, No. 3, Winter 2009–2010, pp. 158–196.

———, *Powerplay: The Origins of the American Alliance System in Asia*, Princeton, N.J.: Princeton University Press, 2016.

Chang, Gordon H., "To the Nuclear Brink: Eisenhower, Dulles, and the Quemoy-Matsu Crisis," *International Security*, Vol. 12, No. 4, Spring 1988, pp. 96–123.

Chanlett-Avery, Emma, *U.S.–South Korea Alliance: Issues for Congress*, Washington, D.C.: Congressional Research Service, IF11388, Version 2, updated June 23, 2020. As of June 3, 2021:
https://crsreports.congress.gov/product/pdf/IF/IF11388

Chiba, Daina, Jesse C. Johnson, and Brett Ashley Leeds, "Careful Commitments: Democratic States and Alliance Design," *Journal of Politics*, Vol. 77, No. 4, October 2015, pp. 968–982.

"China Warns Taiwan Independence 'Means War' as US Pledges Support," BBC News, January 29, 2021. As of September 29, 2021:
https://www.bbc.com/news/world-asia-55851052

Choe Sang-Hun, "U.S. and South Korea Agree to Delay Shift in Wartime Command," *New York Times*, October 24, 2014.

Christensen, Thomas J., *Worse Than a Monolith: Alliance Politics and Problems of Coercive Diplomacy in Asia*, Princeton, N.J.: Princeton University Press, 2011.

Christensen, Thomas J., and Jack Snyder, "Chain Gangs and Passed Bucks: Predicting Alliance Patterns in Multipolarity," *International Organization*, Vol. 44, No. 2, Spring 1990, pp. 137–168.

Colaresi, Michael P., and William R. Thompson, "Hot Spots or Hot Hands? Serial Crisis Behavior, Escalating Risks, and Rivalry," *Journal of Politics*, Vol. 64, No. 4, November 2002, pp. 1175–1198.

Cooley, Alexander, and Daniel Nexon, "Interpersonal Networks and International Security," in Deborah Avant and Oliver Westerwinter, eds., *The New Power Politics: Networks and Transnational Security Governance*, New York: Oxford University Press, 2016, pp. 74–102.

Cooper, Helene, C. J. Chivers, and Clifford J. Levy, "U.S. Watched as a Squabble Turned into a Showdown," *New York Times*, August 17, 2008.

Dafoe, Allan, and Devin Caughey, "Honor and War: Southern US Presidents and the Effects of Concern for Reputation," *World Politics*, Vol. 68, No. 2, April 2016, pp. 341–381.

Drezner, Daniel W., "Just How Entangling Are America's Alliances?" *Washington Post*, August 4, 2015.

Edelstein, David M., and Joshua R. Itzkowitz Shifrinson, "It's a Trap! Security Commitments and the Risks of Entrapment," in A. Trevor Thrall and Benjamin H. Friedman, eds., *US Grand Strategy in the 21st Century*, London: Routledge, 2018, pp. 19–41.

Fang, Songying, Jesse C. Johnson, and Brett Ashley Leeds, "To Concede or to Resist? The Restraining Effect of Military Alliances," *International Organization*, Vol. 68, No. 4, Fall 2014, pp. 775–809.

Foot, Rosemary, *The Wrong War: American Policy and the Dimensions of the Korean Conflict, 1950–1953*, Ithaca, N.Y.: Cornell University Press, 1985.

Fordham, Benjamin, and Paul Poast, "All Alliances Are Multilateral: Rethinking Alliance Formation," *Journal of Conflict Resolution*, Vol. 60, No. 5, 2016, pp. 840–865.

Friedman, Benjamin H., "Bad Idea: Permanent Alliances," Defense360, December 13, 2018. As of July 29, 2021:
https://defense360.csis.org/bad-idea-permanent-alliances/

Gannon, J. Andrés, and Daniel Kent, "Keeping Your Friends Close, but Acquaintances Closer: Why Weakly Allied States Make Committed Coalition Partners," *Journal of Conflict Resolution*, Vol. 65, No. 5, 2021, pp. 889–918.

Garver, John W., *Face Off: China, the United States, and Taiwan's Democratization*, Seattle: University of Washington Press, 1997.

Gavin, Francis J., "Strategies of Inhibition: U.S. Grand Strategy, the Nuclear Revolution, and Nonproliferation," *International Security*, Vol. 40, No. 1, Summer 2015, pp. 9–46.

Gellman, Barton, "U.S. and China Nearly Came to Blows in '96," *Washington Post*, June 21, 1998.

Gertler, Jeremiah, *Operation Odyssey Dawn (Libya): Background and Issues for Congress*, Washington, D.C.: Congressional Research Service, R41725, March 30, 2011. As of June 3, 2021:
https://sgp.fas.org/crs/natsec/R41725.pdf

Gerzhoy, Gene, "Alliance Coercion and Nuclear Restraint: How the United States Thwarted West Germany's Nuclear Ambitions," *International Security*, Vol. 39, No. 4, Spring 2015, pp. 91–129.

Gholz, Eugene, Daryl G. Press, and Harvey M. Sapolsky, "Come Home, America: The Strategy of Restraint in the Face of Temptation," *International Security*, Vol. 21, No. 4, Spring 1997, pp. 5–48.

Glaser, Bonnie S., "Dire Straits: Should American Support for Taiwan Be Ambiguous? A Guarantee Isn't Worth the Risk," *Foreign Affairs*, September 24, 2020. As of August 4, 2021:
https://www.foreignaffairs.com/articles/united-states/2020-09-24/dire-straits

Glaser, John, "Withdrawing from Overseas Bases: Why a Forward-Deployed Military Posture Is Unnecessary, Outdated, and Dangerous," Washington, D.C.: Cato Institute, Policy Analysis No. 816, July 18, 2017.

Glaser, John, Christopher A. Preble, and A. Trevor Thrall, "Towards a More Prudent American Grand Strategy," *Survival*, Vol. 61, No. 5, 2019, pp. 25–42.

Haass, Richard, and David Sacks, "American Support for Taiwan Must Be Unambiguous: To Keep the Peace, Make Clear to China That Force Won't Stand," *Foreign Affairs*, September 2, 2020. As of May 19, 2021: https://www.foreignaffairs.com/articles/united-states/american-support-taiwan-must-be-unambiguous

Henke, Marina E., *Constructing Allied Cooperation: Diplomacy, Payments, and Power in Multilateral Military Coalitions*, Ithaca, N.Y.: Cornell University Press, 2019a.

————, "Buying Allies: Payment Practices in Multilateral Military Coalition-Building," *International Security*, Vol. 43, No. 4, Spring 2019b, pp. 128–162.

————, "Now That Trump Has Abandoned the Kurds, Will Other Countries Ever Trust the U.S.?" *Washington Post*, October 17, 2019c.

Henry, Iain D., "What Allies Want: Reconsidering Loyalty, Reliability, and Alliance Interdependence," *International Security*, Vol. 44, No. 4, Spring 2020, pp. 45–83.

Hubbard, Ben, Charlie Savage, Eric Schmitt, and Patrick Kingsley, "Abandoned by U.S. in Syria, Kurds Find New Ally in American Foe," *New York Times*, updated October 23, 2019.

Jervis, Robert, Keren Yarhi-Milo, and Don Casler, "Redefining the Debate over Reputation and Credibility in International Security: Promises and Limits of New Scholarship," *World Politics*, Vol. 73, No. 1, January 2021, pp. 167–203.

Johnson, Jesse C., "External Threat and Alliance Formation," *International Studies Quarterly*, Vol. 61, No. 3, September 2017, pp. 736–745.

Johnson, Jesse C., and Brett Ashley Leeds, "Defense Pacts: A Prescription for Peace?" *Foreign Policy Analysis*, Vol. 7, No. 1, January 2011, pp. 45–65.

Kadura, Johannes, *The War After the War: The Struggle for Credibility During America's Exit from Vietnam*, Ithaca, N.Y.: Cornell University Press, 2016.

Kagan, Robert, "Superpowers Don't Get to Retire," *New Republic*, May 26, 2014.

Kaiser, David, *American Tragedy: Kennedy, Johnson, and the Origins of the Vietnam War*, Cambridge, Mass.: Harvard University Press, 2000.

Kang, Choong-Nam, "Capability Revisited: Ally's Capability and Dispute Initiation," *Conflict Management and Peace Science*, Vol. 34, No. 5, September 2017, pp. 546–571.

Kavanagh, Jennifer, *U.S. Security-Related Agreements in Force Since 1955: Introducing a New Database*, Santa Monica, Calif.: RAND Corporation, RR-736-AF, 2014. As of August 4, 2021: https://www.rand.org/pubs/research_reports/RR736.html

Kenwick, Michael R., John A. Vasquez, and Matthew A. Powers, "Do Alliances Really Deter?" *Journal of Politics*, Vol. 77, No. 4, October 2015, pp. 943–954.

Keohane, Robert O., "The Big Influence of Small Allies," *Foreign Policy*, No. 2, Spring 1971, pp. 161–182.

Khong, Yuen Foong, *Analogies at War: Korea, Munich, Dien Bien Phu, and the Vietnam Decisions of 1965*, Princeton, N.J.: Princeton University Press, 1992.

Kim, Claudia J., "Military Alliances as a Stabilising Force: U.S. Relations with South Korea and Taiwan, 1950s–1960s," *Journal of Strategic Studies*, Vol. 42, 2019.

Kim, Tongfi, "Why Alliances Entangle but Seldom Entrap States," *Security Studies*, Vol. 20, No. 3, 2011, pp. 350–377.

Kissinger, Henry A., "The Viet Nam Negotiations," *Foreign Affairs*, Vol. 47, No. 2, January 1969, pp. 211–234.

Kreps, Sarah E., *Coalitions of Convenience: United States Military Interventions After the Cold War*, Cambridge, UK: Oxford University Press, 2011.

Lake, David A., *Hierarchy in International Relations*, Ithaca, N.Y.: Cornell University Press, 2011.

Lanoszka, Alexander, "Do Allies Really Free Ride?" *Survival*, Vol. 57, No. 3, 2015, pp. 133–152.

———, *Atomic Assurance: The Alliance Politics of Nuclear Proliferation*, Ithaca, N.Y.: Cornell University Press, 2018a.

———, "Tangled Up in Rose? Theories of Alliance Entrapment and the 2008 Russo-Georgian War," *Contemporary Security Policy*, Vol. 39, No. 2, 2018b, pp. 234–257.

Layne, Christopher, *The Peace of Illusions: American Grand Strategy from 1940 to the Present*, Ithaca, N.Y.: Cornell University Press, 2007.

Leeds, Brett Ashley, "Do Alliances Deter Aggression? The Influence of Military Alliances on the Initiation of Militarized Interstate Disputes," *American Journal of Political Science*, Vol. 47, No. 3, July 2003, pp. 427–439.

Leeds, Brett Ashley, and Jesse C. Johnson, "Theory, Data, and Deterrence: A Response to Kenwick, Vasquez, and Powers," *Journal of Politics*, Vol. 79, No. 1, January 2017, pp. 335–340.

Leeds, Brett, Jeffrey Ritter, Sara Mitchell, and Andrew Long, "Alliance Treaty Obligations and Provisions, 1815–1944," *International Interactions*, Vol. 28, No. 3, 2002, pp. 237–260.

Leffler, Melvyn P., *A Preponderance of Power: National Security, the Truman Administration, and the Cold War*, Stanford, Calif.: Stanford University Press, 1992.

Lind, Jennifer, "Article Review 52 on 'The Myth of Entangling Alliances.' *International Security* 39:4," International Security Studies Forum, ISSF Article Review 52, April 13, 2016.

Logevall, Fredrik, *Choosing War: The Lost Chance for Peace and the Escalation of War in Vietnam*, Berkeley, Calif.: University of California Press, 1999.

———, "The Indochina Wars and the Cold War, 1945–1975," in Melvyn P. Leffler and Odd Arne Westad, eds., *The Cambridge History of the Cold War: Volume II, Crises and Détente*, Cambridge, UK: Cambridge University Press, 2010, pp. 281–304.

———, *Embers of War: The Fall of an Empire and the Making of America's Vietnam*, New York: Random House, 2012.

Machain, Carla Martinez, and T. Clifton Morgan, "The Effect of US Troop Deployment on Host States' Foreign Policy," *Armed Forces & Society*, Vol. 39, No. 1, January 2013, pp. 102–123.

Maoz, Zeev, Paul L. Johnson, Jasper Kaplan, Fiona Ogunkoya, and Aaron Shreve, *Dyadic MID Codebook—Version 4.02*, Davis, Calif.: Department of Political Science, University of California, Davis, June 18, 2021.

Marsh, Kevin, "'Leading from Behind': Neoclassical Realism and Operation Odyssey Dawn," *Defense & Security Analysis*, Vol. 30, No. 2, 2014, pp. 120–132.

Mattes, Michaela, "Reputation, Symmetry, and Alliance Design," *International Organization*, Vol. 66, No. 4, Fall 2012, pp. 679–707.

Mazarr, Michael J., "Dire Straits: Should American Support for Taiwan Be Ambiguous? A Guarantee Won't Solve the Problem," *Foreign Affairs*, September 24, 2020. As of August 4, 2021: https://www.foreignaffairs.com/articles/united-states/2020-09-24/dire-straits

McMahon, Robert J., "Credibility and World Power: Exploring the Psychological Dimension in Postwar American Diplomacy," *Diplomatic History*, Vol. 15, No. 4, Fall 1991, pp. 455–471.

Mearsheimer, John J., and Stephen M. Walt, "The Case for Offshore Balancing: A Superior U.S. Grand Strategy," *Foreign Affairs*, Vol. 95, No. 4, July–August 2016, pp. 70–83.

Mercer, Jonathan, "Emotion and Strategy in the Korean War," *International Organization*, Vol. 67, No. 2, Spring 2013, pp. 221–252.

Miller, Joshua, "Defense Secretary: Libya Did Not Pose Threat to U.S., Was Not 'Vital National Interest' to Intervene," ABC News, March 27, 2011. As of July 29, 2021: https://abcnews.go.com/International/defense-secretary-libya-pose-threat-us-vital-national/story?id=13231987

Miller, Nicholas L., "The Secret Success of Nonproliferation Sanctions," *International Organization*, Vol. 68, No. 4, Fall 2014, pp. 913–944.

———, *Stopping the Bomb: The Sources and Effectiveness of US Nonproliferation Policy*, Ithaca, N.Y.: Cornell University Press, 2018.

Morrow, James D., "Alliances: Why Write Them Down?" *Annual Review of Political Science*, Vol. 3, No. 1, 2000, pp. 63–83.

———, "When Do Defensive Alliances Provoke Rather Than Deter?" *Journal of Politics*, Vol. 79, No. 1, January 2017, pp. 341–345.

Mueller, Karl, "The Demise of Yugoslavia and the Destruction of Bosnia: Strategic Causes, Effects, and Responses," in Robert C. Owen, ed., *Deliberate Force: A Case Study in Effective Air Campaigning*, Maxwell Air Force Base, Ala.: Air University Press, January 2000, pp. 1–36.

Narang, Neil, and Rupal N. Mehta, "The Unforeseen Consequences of Extended Deterrence: Moral Hazard in a Nuclear Client State," *Journal of Conflict Resolution*, Vol. 63, No. 1, 2019, pp. 218–250.

NATO—*See* North Atlantic Treaty Organization.

North Atlantic Treaty Organization, North Atlantic Treaty, April 4, 1949. As of July 30, 2021:
http://www.nato.int/cps/en/natohq/official_texts_17120.htm

Office of Joint History, Office of the Chairman of the Joint Chiefs of Staff, *The Joint Chiefs of Staff and the First Indochina War, 1947–1954*, Washington, D.C.: Joint Chiefs of Staff, 2004.

Palmer, Glenn, Vito D'Orazio, Michael Kenwick, and Matthew Lane, "The MID4 Dataset, 2002–2010: Procedures, Coding Rules and Description," *Conflict Management and Peace Science*, Vol. 32, No. 2, 2015, pp. 222–242.

Palmer, Glenn, and T. Clifton Morgan, *A Theory of Foreign Policy*, Princeton, N.J.: Princeton University Press, 2011.

Posen, Barry R., "Pull Back: The Case for a Less Activist Foreign Policy," *Foreign Affairs*, Vol. 92, No. 1, January–February 2013, pp. 116–128.

———, *Restraint: A New Foundation for U.S. Grand Strategy*, Ithaca, N.Y.: Cornell University Press, 2014.

Press, Daryl G., *Calculating Credibility: How Leaders Assess Military Threats*, Ithaca, N.Y.: Cornell University Press, 2005.

Pressman, Jeremy, *Warring Friends: Alliance Restraint in International Politics*, Ithaca, N.Y.: Cornell University Press, 2008.

Priebe, Miranda, Bryan Rooney, Nathan Beauchamp-Mustafaga, Jeffrey Martini, and Stephanie Pezard, *Implementing Restraint: Changes in U.S. Regional Security Policies to Operationalize a Realist Grand Strategy of Restraint*, Santa Monica, Calif.: RAND Corporation, RR-A739-1, 2021. As of June 4, 2021:
https://www.rand.org/pubs/research_reports/RRA739-1.html

Public Law 96-8, Taiwan Relations Act, January 1, 1979.

Qimao, Chen, "The Taiwan Strait Crisis: Its Crux and Solutions," *Asian Survey*, Vol. 36, No. 11, November 1996, pp. 1055–1066.

Rabinowitz, Or, and Nicholas L. Miller, "Keeping the Bombs in the Basement: U.S. Nonproliferation Policy Toward Israel, South Africa, and Pakistan," *International Security*, Vol. 40, No. 1, Summer 2015, pp. 47–86.

Rapp-Hooper, Mira, *Shields of the Republic: The Triumph and Peril of America's Alliances*, Cambridge, Mass.: Harvard University Press, 2020.

Recchia, Stefano, *Reassuring the Reluctant Warriors: U.S. Civil-Military Relations and Multilateral Intervention*, Ithaca, N.Y.: Cornell University Press, 2015.

Resnick, Evan N., "Hang Together or Hang Separately? Evaluating Rival Theories of Wartime Alliance Cohesion," *Security Studies*, Vol. 22, No. 4, 2013, pp. 672–706.

Romberg, Alan D., *Rein In at the Brink of the Precipice: American Policy Toward Taiwan and U.S.-PRC Relations*, Washington, D.C.: Henry L. Stimson Center, 2003.

Rooney, Bryan, Grant Johnson, and Miranda Priebe, *How Does Defense Spending Affect Economic Growth?* Santa Monica, Calif.: RAND Corporation, RR-A739-2, 2021. As of June 2, 2021:
https://www.rand.org/pubs/research_reports/RRA739-2.html

Ross, Robert S., "The 1995–96 Taiwan Strait Confrontation: Coercion, Credibility, and the Use of Force," *International Security*, Vol. 25, No. 2, Fall 2000, pp. 87–123.

Roulo, Claudette, "Alliances vs. Partnerships," U.S. Department of Defense, March 22, 2019. As of September 29, 2021:
https://www.defense.gov/News/Feature-Stories/story/Article/1684641/alliances-vs-partnerships/

Sayle, Timothy Andrews, *Enduring Alliance: A History of NATO and the Postwar Global Order*, Ithaca, N.Y.: Cornell University Press, 2019.

Schroeder, Paul W., "Alliances, 1815–1945: Weapons of Power and Tools of Management," in Klaus Knorr, ed., *Historical Dimensions of National Security*, Lawrence, Kan.: University Press of Kansas, 1976, pp. 227–262.

Scobell, Andrew, "China and Taiwan: Balance of Rivalry with Weapons of Mass Democratization," *Political Science Quarterly*, Vol. 129, No. 3, Fall 2014, pp. 449–468.

Senese, Paul D., and John A. Vasquez, *The Steps to War: An Empirical Study*, Princeton, N.J.: Princeton University Press, 2008.

Shapiro, Ari, "A Look at the History of the U.S. Alliance with the Kurds," interview with Bilal Wahab on *All Things Considered*, NPR, October 10, 2019. As of June 25, 2021:
https://www.npr.org/2019/10/10/769044811/
a-look-at-the-history-of-the-u-s-alliance-with-the-kurds

Slater, Jerome, "The Domino Theory and International Politics: The Case of Vietnam," *Security Studies*, Vol. 3, No. 2, 1993, pp. 186–224.

Snyder, Glenn H., "The Security Dilemma in Alliance Politics," *World Politics*, Vol. 36, No. 4, July 1984, pp. 461–495.

———, *Alliance Politics*, Ithaca, N.Y.: Cornell University Press, 1997.

Stueck, William, *The Korean War: An International History*, Princeton, N.J.: Princeton University Press, 1995.

———, *Rethinking the Korean War: A New Diplomatic and Strategic History*, Princeton, N.J.: Princeton University Press, 2002.

Suettinger, Robert L., *Beyond Tiananmen: The Politics of U.S.-China Relations 1989–2000*, Washington, D.C.: Brookings Institution Press, 2004.

Sullivan, Eileen, "Trump Questions the Core of NATO: Mutual Defense, Including Montenegro," *New York Times*, July 18, 2018.

Thrall, A. Trevor, and Caroline Dorminey, *Risky Business: The Role of Arms Sales in U.S. Foreign Policy*, Washington, D.C.: Cato Institute, Policy Analysis No. 836, March 13, 2018.

Toal, Gerard, *Near Abroad: Putin, the West, and the Contest over Ukraine and the Caucasus*, Oxford, UK: Oxford University Press, 2017.

Trachtenberg, Marc, *A Constructed Peace: The Making of the European Settlement, 1945–1963*, Vol. 79, Princeton, N.J.: Princeton University Press, 1999.

U.S. Department of State, "U.S. Collective Defense Arrangements," webpage, undated. As of October 4, 2021:
https://2009-2017.state.gov/s/l/treaty/collectivedefense/index.htm

U.S. Senate, A Resolution Strongly Condemning the Gross and Systematic Violations of Human Rights in Libya, Including Violent Attacks on Protesters Demanding Democratic Reforms, and for Other Purposes, Bill 85, March 1, 2011.

Walt, Stephen M., *The Origins of Alliance*, Ithaca, N.Y.: Cornell University Press, 1987.

———, *Taming American Power: The Global Response to U.S. Primacy*, New York: W. W. Norton & Company, 2006.

———, "How to Tell If You're in a Good Alliance," *Foreign Policy*, October 28, 2019.

Weisiger, Alex, and Keren Yarhi-Milo, "Revisiting Reputation: How Past Actions Matter in International Politics," *International Organization*, Vol. 69, No. 2, Spring 2015, pp. 473–495.

Weitsman, Patricia A., *Dangerous Alliances: Proponents of Peace, Weapons of War*, Stanford, Calif.: Stanford University Press, 2004.

Yarhi-Milo, Keren, Alexander Lanoszka, and Zack Cooper, "To Arm or to Ally? The Patron's Dilemma and the Strategic Logic of Arms Transfers and Alliances," *International Security*, Vol. 41, No. 2, Fall 2016, pp. 90–139.